Fenland Waterways

A backwater at St. Ives

A Pictorial Anthology by
ALAN ROULSTONE
Text by
MICHAEL ROULSTONE

FIRST EDITION 1974

BALFOUR PUBLICATIONS (PHOTO PRECISION LTD.)
ST. IVES, HUNTINGDON
ISBN 085944 021 4

CONTENTS

FOREWORD

The compilers of this 'anthology' are fully aware that two charges may well be levelled against them. Firstly, that they have not defined Fenland's boundaries with any degree of accuracy; secondly, that their choice of subject matter could well be altered or varied in numerous ways. To the first of these charges the only possible defence lies in the form of a question: who can truly explain where Fenland begins and where it ends? To the second the compilers can only advance the privilege that is common to all compilers of anthologies: that the term itself denotes selection, and the more personal that selection is the better.

Having said that, the compilers must also make two other points. The first is that this book is not intended to be a manual or guide for those who wish to spend a holiday afloat in the fens. The second is that limitations of space have inevitably precluded the illustration and description of a multiplicity of intriguing subjects, so that this book presents only a limited choice from among Fenland's many attractions.

The plan followed is the simple one of tracing the courses of the navigable waterways to be discovered in Fenland. Thus, beginning at Bedford, the Ouse is followed downstream as far as the Wash, and then the Witham is pursued upstream as far as Lincoln. After that the imaginary navigator is made to return down the Witham to the Wash and explore in turn the Welland and the Nene, finally retracing his course to the Wash along the old Nene. Certain other navigable Fenland waterways are also explored in the course of the narrative, thereby allowing a wide-ranging consideration of the places of interest to be found beside these rivers, whether natural or man-made.

Author and illustrator, both of them one-time residents in the northern part of the area and wholly appreciative of the character of Fenland, would like to take this opportunity to commend this part of England to those who are as yet unacquainted with it. The publication is not intended exclusively for the water-borne holiday-maker; it is designed to prove of equal interest to the motorist or anybody else who has derived pleasure from a visit to the fens, and it is hoped the book will be thought a worthy souvenir of time passed pleasantly in this part of the country.

6

The A 6 crosses the Ouse at Bedford

INTRODUCTORY

The Ouse — not the Ouse in Yorkshire — but the Great Ouse that flows through Bedfordshire, Huntingdonshire, Cambridgeshire and even parts of Norfolk; the Nene, originating in its present guise deep in the Midlands and flowing obstinately to the Wash, the greater part of its final course being man-devised; the Welland, only navigable for a short stretch; some few miles of the Cam; and finally the Witham that cuts deep into Lincolnshire; these are the main waterways mentioned in these pages, together with such tributaries and connected channels formed by the hand of man as are navigable. Fenland has been taken to extend from Lincoln in the north down to Bedford in the south and across country eastwards as far as the sea (the Wash) at one extreme and the city of Cambridge at the other.

The history of Fenland, as it is hoped is sufficiently stressed in the following pages, is the history of drainage, and more recently of agriculture. The most surprising factor of all is that this drainage, although it can be traced back to Roman times and, later, to the monks of the middle ages, dates principally from the early seventeenth century, modern Fenland's formative age. Charles I was invited to take an active interest in the cutting of new waterways and the reclamation of land. Cromwell, who hailed from this part of the country, tended to overlook such matters; perhaps he apprehended the mercenary nature of those who wished to drain the fens. Charles II, like his father before him, was obliged to interest himself in Fenland but throughout the Carolean era the name of one man, a man possessed with the problems of land reclamation, the digging of new channels, the pumping of water by artificial means from one place to another, stood supreme. It was that of the Dutchman Vermuyden, Sir Cornelius Vermuyden in later life, contemporary of another great Dutchman who became an English knight, Sir Anthony Van Dyck. The tenaciousness of purpose that was evidently common to both men positively leaps from the pages of books written by those who have taken an interest in Vermuyden's achievements. He must surely qualify as one of the greatest engineers ever to have practised in Britain; and it is partly due to his endeavours that Fenland is peaceful today, its waters safely navigable.

He was responsible first of all for what is today called the 'Old Bedford River'; later, after peat shrinkage and a consequent lowering of the level of land had shown this to be unsatisfactory, he became even bolder and proposed the 'Hundred Foot Drain' (one hundred feet in width), now known as the 'New Bedford River', running parallel to the earlier channel, together with such additional 'cuts' and 'drains' as were thought necessary. This 'New Bedford', it has to be remembered, is just over twenty miles in length, one hundred feet in width and sufficiently deep to be navigable by all such craft as wished originally to take advantage of it. It was a 'drain', nothing more. The cutting of it, the construction of its colossal banks, was a considerable enterprise. The tidal Ouse south of Kings Lynn had to be contended with at one extreme, the undisciplined 'Old West River' at the other. The problem of future peat shrinkage had to be faced. One is accustomed to reading of nineteenth century enterprises of this kind; but all of this took place two centuries earlier. Poor Vermuyden was disrespected in his own lifetime, mistrusted for being a foreigner. Fenland, at least in its southern reaches, is however largely Vermuyden land — even if the three drainage areas or 'levels' into which the fens are conveniently divided bear the name of 'Bedford' after the scheme's sponsor.

Vermuyden's fens and Vermuyden's endeavours do not however constitute all of Fenland and its history; even if it is a fact that hardly one of the inland waterways mentioned in the following pages, with the sole exception of the twisting Witham, would be navigable today were it not for his one-time exertions, hare-brained as they were sometimes considered to be. Northern Fenland — Roman Fenland — is totally different. The terrain is different, the people are different; yet over the years its struggle has been precisely similar, and the richness of its soil today is the same as that further south, in that expansive no-man's land that surrounds the town of Chatteris for instance.

Although the northern part of the fens is further removed from London and the south of England, it somehow appears to have more contact with the everyday world than do places that are nearer. What has happened is that the Great North Road has, for as many centuries as man in the south has wished to convene with man in the north, pursued a thrustful path directly to the west of the fens, hardly ever touching them, except perhaps at Stamford which lies right on their perimeter, or at Grantham, which properly belongs to Fenland for the agricultural richness of its surrounding countryside but cannot be mentioned in these pages (despite its magnificent church) because it does not lie beside navigable water; and somehow the fens to the north have had greater contact with this road than those to the south. Possibly in part because of this it is no accident that the ecclesiastical city of Lincoln is larger and its cathedral marginally finer than Ely, the corresponding Fenland city to the south.

Fenland's principal identity emanates from the Wash, a menacing stretch of water that even to this day is only prevented by man's sheer determination from submerging acre upon acre of good agricultural land. It is muddy, unattractive and virtually unapproachable, surrounded by dank clay and jutting inland as though it considered itself an emphatic spade attacking an herbaceous border. It is extremely dangerous to navigate (and a pilot should always be employed); yet its ever-changing shape, attended by several natural and man-made channels, is somehow in character with Fenland.

If all this sounds a little unappetising perhaps it will be considered allowable to end this brief introduction with the following lines from Michael Drayton on the 'Pleasures of the Fennes':

> *The toyling* Fisher *here is tewing of his Net:*
> *The* Fowler *is imployed his lymed twigs to set.*
> *One underneath his Horse, to get a shoot doth stalke;*
> *Another over Dykes upon his Stilts doth walke:*
> *There other with their Spades, the Peats are squaring out,*
> *And others from their Canes, are busily about,*
> *To draw out Sedge and Reed, for Thatch and Stover fit,*
> *That whosoever would a Landskip rightly hit,*
> *Beholding but my Fennes, shall with more shapes be stor'd,*
> *Then* Germany, *or* France, *or* Thuscan *can afford:*
> *And for that part of me, which men high* Holland *call,*
> *Where* Boston *seated is, by plenteous* Wythams *fall,*
> *I peremptory am, large* Neptunes *liquid field,*
> *Doth to no other tract the like abundance yeeld.*

10

The Embankment, Bedford

CHAPTER ONE

From Bedford to the Cam

The traveller passing through Bedford on his way across country towards the west of England is hardly aware that the old county town so intimately associated with John Bunyan, the gentle clerical author of *The Pilgrim's Progress,* stands on a river at all. It does, and the prospect across the water once he has taken the trouble to look for it is most pleasing. But above and beyond both these factors, at least among boating enthusiasts, is the fact that Bedford is rapidly becoming one of the most important boating centres on the Great Ouse. It is now provided with an extremely well-appointed and unusually attractive marina; and although much remains still to be accomplished in the task of making the stretch of water running east out of Bedford into what will ultimately be an easily navigable waterway once more, after several years of neglect, work is already well advanced and the river between Bedford and St. Neots should soon be as amenable to the contemporary boatman as that between St. Neots and Huntingdon, itself surely one of the loveliest stretches of waterway in all of Fenland, as even travellers by rail passing this way in summer will readily testify.

The Ouse from Bedford to Huntingdon, and beyond through St. Ives to Ely, perhaps epitomises what the boating enthusiast means when he waxes enthusiastic about Fenland rivers, and it would be difficult not to concur with his enthusiasm. Before parting company with Bedford and proceeding with this of necessity rapid glance at Fenland's navigable waterways it would perhaps be well to cast a thought in the direction of the genius-possessed clergyman whose memory today provides this traffic-ridden town with one of its principal associations of interest. Happily, travellers on the Ouse are in a position to appreciate John Bunyan with a greater degree of tranquillity than motorists can allow themselves.

Bunyan was born at Elstow, and the old half-timbered grammar school which he attended there is still intact. Even though the village now verges on the outspreading suburbia about Bedford it is still peaceful and fitting for the home of a man so undeniably good, even if he was somewhat unworldly, steeped in the language and morality of the 'authorised version' of the Old Testament. He did not stray far from his beloved Bedfordshire, and indeed the countryside about here is to this day know as 'Bunyan country'. It was as a result of his Puritan leanings and the eventual overthrow of the Cromwellian usurpers that he passed an extended period in Bedford Gaol, the door of which is today preserved in the vestibule of the Bunyan

Meeting House which was built in 1850 and also contains a Bunyan museum. It was in this gaol that he wrote *The Pilgrim's Progress*, which begins with the famous allusion to his incarceration there: 'As I walk'd through the wilderness of this world, I lighted on a certain place where was a Den, and I laid me down in that place to sleep; and as I slept, I dreamed a Dream...'. As they pass by or through this town and observe Bunyan's statue, present-day travellers and holiday makers might well pause to remember his unwearying devotion to what he believed to be right.

Once he has left Bedford the waterways pilgrim pursues a tranquil course — or will soon be in a position to do so — through a series of locks as far as Tempsford, travelling almost due east. At Tempsford the river makes off in a northerly direction; it is here also that the River Ivel — itself no longer in navigable condition — joins with the Ouse. Biggleswade and Hitchin lie due south of here beside the Ivel, both of them acting today partly as dormitory towns for Greater London; and this fact in itself is a hint to the Londoner that the peaceful waterways of Fenland are not too very far distant from his office or, if he happens to commute from the north of London, his home. Indeed, this is something that Londoners are becoming aware of in ever increasing numbers, transforming the area surrounding Huntingdon and St. Ives into a cosmopolitan boating enthusiasts' mecca, devotees speeding there regularly for a weekend's relaxation afloat.

It is difficult to say where, to the south, the fens actually begin; it is not very easy, in fact, to arrive at a satisfactory and all-embracing definition of Fenland. In this instance the town of Bedford has been selected as a convenient place of embarkation, but surely, as far as the waterways are concerned, it is to the north of St. Neots that Fenland may truly be said to begin — though Fenland natives, experts or purists, will aver that it is at Over, to the east even of St. Ives, that the fens really begin.

Fenland is flat but it is not monotonous and sometimes during the evening it possesses an elemental serenity, when expansive skies unperturbed by thrustful uplands or extensive areas of obscuring woodland, take on their full glory, providing the gazer with an ever-varying spectrum of pink and purple.

Following the course of the Ouse between St. Neots and Huntingdon, true Fenland character is only just perceptibly in evidence. There is still a too preponderant luxuriance of vegetation to be seen on either side of the river. Wild fowl — as indeed is the case throughout the fens — are to be observed in abundance, although here, unlike the fens further to the east, most striking are the herons immobile in the shallows or beside the banks awaiting the approach of subaqueous prey. This is lovely country, and the increasing volume of river traffic shows that it is appreciated.

Today St. Neots is a small industrial town, one of many to have enjoyed the prosperity that has followed the overspill of population from London. Its name still

The Bridge Hotel, St. Neots

has the power to remind the curious of an era as long ago as the twelfth century, of the year 1130, in which St. Neot, then but an ordinary monk from Glastonbury, the cradle of English monasticism, became head of a monastery here. Neot was a contemporary of King Alfred, and indeed had once been his tutor.

Ancient associations are widespread throughout the area, and often stretch back in time much further than the days of St. Neot. Close by runs the Roman Ermine Street, one of those enterprising straight roads that even in an age of heavy traffic congestion such as has arisen today will allow one the solitudinous and often intensely personal pleasure of musing upon the doings of past generations; of marvelling at the might, efficiency and sheer determination of those ancient conquerors, who left as suddenly as they came and curiously, apart it is said from the London cockneys, left no trace of their blood at all in English veins.

In nearby Buckden, to the north of St. Neots and just removed from the river, there stands an interesting survivor from earlier times in the form of a palace built for the Bishops of Lincoln during the late fifteenth century. Today the remains of this structure are employed as a school. A startling contrast to the antiquity of this institution is provided by the modernity of Buckden Marina, on the river itself. This amenity was opened as recently as 1971 and boasts the honour of having then been awarded a 'Countryside Award', to commemorate 'European Conservation Year' and in recognition of what is described on one of the plaques shown here as an 'outstanding contribution to the countryside'.

Ermine Street ran from London to Lincoln, passing through Huntingdon and crossing the Ouse at the lovely but exceedingly irritating narrow bridge that divides Huntingdon from Godmanchester, a lovely little borough of great antiquity, now incorporated with Huntingdon. Like Bedford, Huntingdon is a county town, not a city. During recent years it has allowed itself to become somewhat unpleasing in appearance, a rather untidily sprawling place in some respects but with many good points in addition to the graceful river that flows beside it.

Oliver Cromwell, born nearby, attended the Huntingdon grammar school, which has now been converted into a Cromwell museum where one might ponder perhaps upon the great might this Huntingdonshire native achieved in national life, only to have it destroyed posthumously and anti-climactically after the Restoration, when his remains were exhumed from their resting place in Westminster Abbey and the dismembered head was placed on a pike outside the old Palace of Westminster in London.

Opposite Cromwell's old school in Huntingdon there is a small churchyard, and possibly there is equal food for thought in the words inscribed on an old gravestone that is today placed prominently against the church wall. The stone commemorates the passing in 1774 of one Thomas Jetherel, a local maltster and corn merchant who was unfortunate enough, as this gravestone frankly informs whoever is still

14

Buckden Marina

interested in such matters, to be declared bankrupt. Recording this sorry trifle of local information, the inscription triumphantly concludes: 'That, if he scandalised the world by some miscarriages; he hath instructed it, by repairing them, to the utmost of his power. Who chose rather to leave his relations in want, than transmit to them a patrimony of malediction; and give them an example of equity rather than the fruit of injustice'. What a hidden story either of smugness or of stubbornness is contained within those engraved words. 'Go thou and do likewise', the stone charges the passer-by.

But perhaps the passer-by will be more tempted to review the implications of this solemn record over a glass of beer; and well advised he would be, for Huntingdon is admirably provided to see to his requirements in this respect. The old 'George Hotel', a one-time coaching inn with its galleried courtyard still intact, should by no means be overlooked. It has still remembered associations from the Second World War with both the British Red Cross and the American armed forces. Nor should the 'Feathers Inn' in the market place be overlooked, but it is the 'Old Bridge Hotel' beside the river, taking its name from the 1332 bridge, that will appeal most immediately to the boating enthusiast, a pleasingly luxurious establishment in which to escape from the sheer hard work that boating entails. If one so wishes, it is possible to sit outside here at leisure and calmly watch the river activity and the swans serenely journeying to or from neighbouring Godmanchester. Or, pityingly, one can watch the jostle of cars and lorries attempting to negotiate the historic bridge which it is to be hoped will never be replaced in the interest of progress.

Huntingdon has long been a prosperous town, and the nearby presence of United States Army Air Force bases has only tended to heighten this circumstance. It is in the outlying villages, though, that the true outlet of this affluence has been felt; in the hasty increases imposed upon the cost of housing, for instance, and in the 'executive' character that seems all at once to have pervaded them, delightful as they still are to stroll through, redolent even yet of peaceful times gone by and happily still not completely obscured.

To pass beside the neighbouring villages by boat should be doubly satisfying. Leaving Huntingdon, whose lovely bridge Daniel Defoe in the seventeenth century thought 'a very great ornament to the place' — a sentiment most motorists today would vehemently and impatiently dispute — the Ouse passes firstly by Hartford, now efficiently blessed with a large marina, and then to the overlapping villages of Wyton and Houghton. The fens proper still lie to the east, though the surrounding country here is flat and the fields far larger in size than further west beyond Bedford. The Ouse winds pleasantly, its current almost sluggish; boats must take care to keep to the centre of the river, for it is narrow here and plentifully provided on either bank with reeds that are harvested annually, although it is forbidden for the public to gather them.

The Old Bridge at Huntingdon

17

18   *Swans on the Ouse at Godmanchester*

Despite the narrowness and seeming shallowness, it is surprising to be reminded that boating enthusiasts from as far north as Goole in Yorkshire are, by the connecting agency of the extremely tricky Wash, enabled to enter the Ouse at Kings Lynn and sail as far as St. Ives and beyond. As a glance at a map will demonstrate, there are numerous variations to this enterprising exercise.

It is along the stretch of river that flows between Huntingdon and Ely that the traditional English waterside inn seems to play such a major part in pleasing both boatmen and more conventional voyagers and adventurers — for what can be more pleasing to the tired motorist, on a pleasant summer's day or evening, than to stand or sit upon the terrace of an inn beside the river and simply watch the water and its boats? At Wyton there is the fine old 'Three Jolly Butchers'. It possesses today only a somewhat dilapidated landing stage, and it requires its river patrons to walk several yards from their boats before entering, but once inside the reward well recompenses the effort; for this is one of the very best public houses in this part of the country, dating from the seventeenth century and displaying the remnants of contemporary mural decorations on its walls.

Wyton and Houghton run into one another, pleasantly removed from the very busy road running between Huntingdon and St. Ives. Life seems to move at an extremely leisurely pace in these two villages from which it is possible, in not much above half an hour, to walk by footpath, much of it beside the river, into St. Ives, a pleasing exercise during the summer months, matched only by the unhurried journey thither by river, passing by the villages of Hemingford Abbots and Hemingford Grey on the opposite side of the water. At the first of these is to be found the 'Axe and Compass', yet another attractive inn.

The old mill at Houghton, today the property of the National Trust and rented to the Youth Hostels Association, is thought to be the oldest watermill still standing on the Great Ouse, though it operates no more and its mill wheel has vanished with the passage of the years. Its situation is delightful and it has been gratifyingly well preserved, an impressive monument to a past age.

Hemingford Grey lies on the opposite, or the southern side of the Ouse. Its lovely village church, unmistakable for its octagonally topped tower, strikes one immediately. At one time this church boasted a spire, but high winds demolished most of it in 1741, and all that remains is the present immediately identifiable stump.

Beyond the Hemingfords there is pastureland to the right and what is called the 'thicket' to the left. Swans grace the river — traditional Fenland birds — and in clement weather strollers are to be seen along both banks. An air of quietude prevails, punctuated from time to time by the chugging of boat engines. Suddenly, travelling east, the borough of St. Ives comes into view, the first of its two church spires visible above the houses, though its famous bridge is not in sight until one has

Houghton Mill

reached the very centre of the little town, after passing a flower bedecked river bank known as the 'Waits'.

The first of St. Ives' two spired churches is the parish church, which possesses one of the most peaceful churchyards to be chanced upon anywhere, with the river flowing past beneath it. At some time during the nineteenth century, there must have lived at St. Ives a stone-mason with unusually ambitious leanings. A large number of the gravestones here boast cherubic faces carved in bas-relief, emblematic foliage and gracious classical decoration, all obviously the work of one and the same man, or at least his workshop. This form of 'folk art' is to be observed everywhere; but there are areas in this country where the tread of progress has been slower than elsewhere and where consequent desecration has not had the same marked effect. Often enough the labours of the old time stone-mason produced poor results, but here the outcome was first class and is still worthy of passing attention. The spire of the parish church is not original. It was rebuilt after an early aviator crashed into it at the time of the First World War, himself perishing, and destroying the spire at the same time.

In the town there are still two former coaching inns, and was it not at St. Ives — this St. Ives, not that once attractive town of the same name in Cornwall — that a man was actually so audacious as to acquire seven wives?

As a trading centre this small town has always been of great importance as far as the Fenland farmer is concerned. It still is, and each Monday there is a busy cattle and also a general market here, while on Bank Holidays the town is invaded by literally thousands of strangers who come looking for bargains at its nationally famous fair which originated in the twelfth century. To the farmer it is St. Ives, rather than Huntingdon, which is the important 'local' town in this area; even if the trains no longer run as far as St. Ives.

St. Ives also claims Cromwellian associations, and a statue of the Great Protector, who was formerly a farmer nearby, stands in the centre of this prosperous little town. It possesses too a chapel on its bridge, though it is no longer in use and no longer boasts the upper storey it once had. Dedicated to St. Leger, it is one of only two such buildings in England, the other being at Wakefield (although what is known as the 'lock-up' at Bradford-on-Avon used also to be a chapel on a bridge). Doubtless the so-called 'powers that be' would relish the opportunity to replace this narrow fifteenth century bridge in order to render the gateway to the Cambridge road more easily negotiable, but with good fortune they will never be allowed their way. The bridge is one of Huntingdonshire's most unusual features, a source of constant wonderment to travellers both by road and river.

If one stands on the bridge, in one of the bays that flank the chapel, and looks downstream, the prospect of a meandering river with rich green meadows to either side is irresistible. Visible in the distance is the lovely village of Holywell, a village

Hemingford Grey

The Chapel on the Bridge, St. Ives 23

without a shop (its official name is Holywell-cum-Needingworth, the latter village lying just up the road). Looking to the south side of the river from the bridge, one's gaze follows the direction of the road to Cambridge, a mere half hour's drive or less away by car, standing beside another Fenland river, to be glanced at a little later in these pages.

As a village Holywell is indeed one of the treasures of southern Fenland with trim cottages looking out towards the river. During the winter the winds, and during the wetter months the rains, can render this part of Fenland bleak and un-amenable but during the spring and summer it is delightful. The 'Old Ferry Boat Inn' — its very name reminding patrons of the not so distant past when ferries across the river existed in profusion, faces the river at one end of the village with the church standing back from the river at the opposite extremity.

This publication is not intended to be a chronicle of the attractive waterside public houses to be discovered in the fens — at any rate not disproportionately so — but it would be unfair not to mention in passing the fact that the 'Old Ferry Boat' is among the contenders for the unresolvable title of oldest inn in England. That it is also among the better such establishments, not only in the fens but in the whole country, only adds to its interest to the traveller.

Low beams characterise the interior of this excellent hostelry, but another intriguing feature is its claim to be haunted: not by an unfriendly ghost but by that of a young woman by the name of Juliet who committed suicide some nine hundred years ago, the victim of an unrequited love for a local woodcutter. The inn, so it is averred, stands on the site of her grave, and every March 17 her ghost is said to appear. There are local people who will try to persuade you that this legend is fact, who claim to have been aware of Juliet's presence on this day of the year. For those of a less romantic turn of mind perhaps the information that the 'Old Ferry Boat' is known to have been retailing liquor as early as the year 968 provides a stronger incentive to visit it.

Having gained the 'Old Ferry Boat' the sailor in this direction may fittingly congratulate himself upon at last having penetrated the fens as they are understood by Fenlanders. It is true that even here people employ the phrase 'out in the fens' to convey the information that this is a place far removed from the scenically less interesting, but at the same time agriculturally rich terrain of the fens; but a glance at the map should be sufficient to remind one how very tenuous and technical their argument is. They will point to superficially impoverished looking farmers and assure you, not without an air of mystery, that these gentlemen come from 'out in the fens'. They may well inform you at the same time that the objects of their talk are what they term 'land millionaires'; hastily they will add the qualifying remark that in the fens being such a mortal means nothing at all really, certainly does not indicate that the landowner in question enjoys the kind of affluence normally

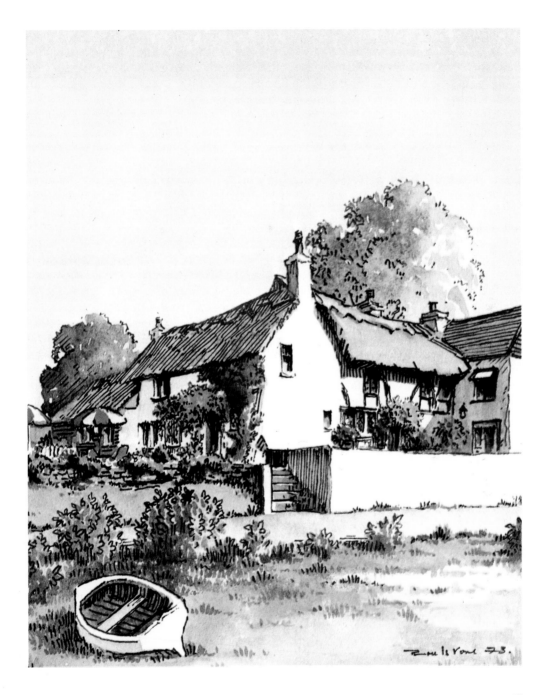

The Old Ferry Boat Inn, Holywell

25

accompanying the lives of such outwardly wealthy beings. What they mean to convey by statements such as this is not so much the fact that the possessors of numerous Fenland acres are less well off than their counterparts in other parts of the country, but rather that farming in the fens is a precarious occupation, one that can just as easily yield bitter distress as anything else.

This is another story, however. At Holywell, and even beyond, one is still only on the fringe of Fenland. Between Holywell and Earith (where, incidentally, there is another fine riverside inn) there lies the area of flatland commonly known as the Ouse Fen. At Earith also are to be found the southern ends of the Old and New Bedford Rivers, both of them navigable and both conveying a sense of near legendary and heroic impressiveness. Here indeed, for he who would contemplate the lasting and at times soul-destroying fight to preserve Fenland from the waters, is food for thought.

The story of the quest to utilise the land to fruitful ends is a long one, extending back in time for as long as man has inhabited the fens, or at any rate cultivated them, however partially. It encompasses two distinct endeavours: reclamation and drainage, and neither battle may be said to have been won as yet. The great era of drainage may be assigned to Carolean times, the seventeenth century; the names of a Duke of Bedford and of Cornelius Vermuyden are the two most significant, the former in the guise of entrepreneur, head of a group of investors or 'adventurers', the latter a Dutchman, possessed by the desire to do for the fens what had already been undertaken and in large part accomplished in the Low Countries.

That Vermuyden was a foreigner and largely unsuccessful in his initial efforts were two factors held against him in his lifetime; the deposing of Charles I and Cromwell's assumption of power led to his being temporarily deprived of the opportunity to continue with his work. Before his time Fenland life and cultivation, such as it was, had been one of incredible hardihood; there exist tales even of men being obliged to walk about on stilts, of houses being built on stilts. Even down to the present day people have had to resort to cunning in order to match their wits against the elements and to overcome the discomforts and tragedies of flooding. The expansive fields of black soil one sees today in the fens, covering acre upon acre of land, were in the past subject to regular flooding, in certain instances permanent; while further east there was no true land at all, properly speaking, and as every reader of the story of Hereward the Wake is aware, the Isle of Ely was almost literally an island.

Today much of the land lies dangerously below sea level; the straight, high-banked 'cuts' of the Old and New Bedford Rivers and the numerous cuts and 'drains' bearing such names as the 'Forty Foot', names commensurate with their width, flow artificially across the land, and to drive along beneath one of these banks, along a narrow, dead-straight road with the nearby 'river' level possibly

Overcote Ferry and the Pike and Eel

above one's head, is an almost alarming experience. Widespread Fenland flooding has occurred several times during the present century, usually because of exceptionally high levels of rainfall. The mere existence of these drains is in itself daunting enough; the frequent sluices, or floodgates, and the numerous small but powerful pumping stations to be observed throughout the fens, are permanent reminders of the potential dangers inherent in living and working in this part of the country.

Even more salutary is the reflection that Fenland soil is shrinking, its height above sea level — if at all — ever decreasing, especially where peat is prevalent. It requires men to apply their minds permanently to the problem of arming themselves with defences against the water. If over the years this continuing battle, at the outset simply for the means of livelihood and in more recent times for the accoutrements of ordinary civilised English life, has inbred in the minds of fen people an indomitable stubbornness and doggedness it is hardly surprising. The traveller by water, as he pauses perhaps at the excellent 'Pike and Eel' hotel just before he reaches Earith, would do well to remember this. In part, the privilege he is allowed of enjoying his holiday or day afloat has come about only through the endeavours of dedicated men and women over a period that embraces centuries.

At Earith he will receive positive proof of this; for in addition to the lock that grants him access to the Old West River, as the ensuing stretch of the Great Ouse is known, he will encounter the seven arches of the Earith Sluice. The straight cuts of the New and Old Bedfords lead off into the distance, the first of them no longer navigable for the first part of its course, but only from nearby Mepal. Both of them rejoin the Ouse at Denver Sluice, that lordly triumph of early engineering skill, a distance of over thirty miles away. Both rivers are man-made, entirely lacking in scenic interest, but a cause of wonderment simply for the reminder they give of the struggle their construction incurred.

The Old Bedford was begun about 1634, taking some three years to complete. It did not prove to be altogether successful, for it failed to take land shrinkage into account, and for this reason Vermuyden, later Sir Cornelius, who had already met with bitter opposition in England, was commissioned to suggest further plans for urgently necessary drainage, resulting among other things in the cutting of the 'Hundred Foot' drain, the New Bedford River, constructed between 1650 and 1651, joining up with the Ouse again at Denver, and in practice rendering the surviving stretch of the Ouse between Earith and Denver no more than a supplementary drain to Vermuyden's great channel.

This is by no means the entire story of the drainage of the southern fens. Such is not the purpose of this short book, and it has been feelingly recorded elsewhere on many occasions, most notably in H. C. Darby's *The Draining of the Fens;* but anybody who has had an opportunity to look at Vermuyden's cuts will at any rate

Through the Locks at Earith

receive some intimation of the vastness of the enterprise, one moreover that took place at a time when feats of engineering of this kind were far more arduous of accomplishment than would be the case today. One conjures up an image of Vermuyden as of a man possessed, demoniac in his application to his assumed task. But it should not pass unregarded that Francis, fourth Earl of Bedford, and William, the fifth Earl and first Duke, who headed the enterprise, were enthusiastic for one reason only: not to alleviate the suffering of Fenlanders but to line their own pockets and acquire additional, reclaimed acres. It is not surprising that the scheme met with a good deal of opposition, though admittedly this was partly because Fenlanders were not convinced of the efficiency of the Dutch engineer's plans, and despised him moreover, as is the case with many insular peoples, for not being one of their own kind.

Fenland farmers today, however, even though they have to contend with what are in many ways unacceptable conditions, are able to enjoy the advantages of tilling some of the most fertile soil in Great Britain; thick, black, moist soil, capable of yielding root crops, corn and, as further north, flowers in overwhelming super-abundance. Sheep and cattle too benefit from the lush growth of grass in this corner of the country. It is far indeed from being a 'depressed area', even if it seems a somewhat unforthcoming one. As every Fenland gardener will tell you, the weeds that blight his flowerbeds are unsurmountably fertile.

The Old West River beyond Earith, with its high banks as protection against flooding, was once a far more turbulent stretch of water than it is today; the Bedford Rivers have relieved it of much of its burden. The boating enthusiast may pass along it in comfort and safety, making in the direction of what is known as Pope's Corner, where the Cam joins with the Ouse, and where the Ouse reassumes its own proper nomenclature, calling itself the Ely Ouse for a short while. Here the gourmandising traveller will find himself beside an establishment known as the 'Fish and Duck'. Today this is an attractive and very popular eating house — not a pub in the ordinary sense of the word, but essentially a restaurant — but with a history that extends back centuries, to the thirteenth century when the monastery at Ely was such a flourishing establishment and this was but a humble ale house. It is said that monks from Ely used to come here frequently, and certainly there is no reason to question the assertion.

Before closing this chapter in order to explore a little of the Cam — at least as far to the south as Cambridge, which is as far in that direction as one should decently glance when thinking in terms of the fens — it is worthwhile mentioning very briefly the stretch of the Old West that lies between Earith and the Cam.

There is not very much of interest to be observed here, not from an historical point of view; but the surrounding countryside is rich agriculturally, and the land to be observed on either side of the river is pure Fenland. Celery is an important crop at

Where Waterways Meet — The Fish and Duck

Stretham, just a little removed from the river; and the old Roman Akeman Street, now the A.10, crosses the Ouse nearby to run more or less parallel with the Cam south to Cambridge. From Cambridge a further Roman road extends in a south-westerly direction to join up with Ermine Street, already mentioned in these pages in connection with Huntingdon, through which it also passes. Ely lies on the Ouse north of Stretham, set upon an eminence that until a century or so ago looked out over an expanse of flatland speckled with literally scores of windmills. Most of these have now gone, replaced in the first instance by steam pumping stations and then by the more efficient oil-driven mechanical pumps one sees today, Fenland's own characteristic symbol of self-reassurance.

CHAPTER TWO

From Cambridge to Kings Lynn

The River Cam is a delightful and important feature of the historic university city of Cambridge. As it wanders through the town, changing its name from Granta to Cam at the Silver Street Bridge, it carries with it an atmosphere of calm relaxation that the Thames, perhaps on account of its greater size, is not quite able to achieve at Oxford. Once busy with barge traffic plying between Cambridge and Kings Lynn, today the river is more likely to be carrying punts, 'eights' and motor cruisers, all of them pursuing pleasure rather than commerce.

Cambridge is a lovely city, and many of its colleges and churches are architectural treasures, of which there is space here only briefly to mention one or two, including King's College Chapel, one of the most perfect structures in the Perpendicular style to be found anywhere in England. It has been well cleaned in recent years, its interior now light and wholly satisfying, described by Wordsworth as 'this immense and glorious work of fine intelligence'. Its lofty walls, graceful arches and superb ceiling are all to be wondered at, the fine yellow-brown of its mellowed walls an exquisite sight and conducive to meditative admiration.

Before leaving Cambridge it would be wrong not to visit also the famous Round Church of the Holy Sepulchre. Four only of these curious structures survive in England today, all of them built either by the Knights Templars or by the Knights Hospitallers, members of medieval orders of chivalry with quasi-monastic ideals included among their articles of faith. They were designed to resemble in token fashion the Church of the Holy Sepulchre in Jerusalem. It is an architectural curio most tourists visit, and the boating visitor should not fail to do likewise.

Nearby Grantchester, on the Cam just to the south of Cambridge, reminds one of Rupert Brooke's much quoted lines:

> *Stands the Church clock at ten to three?*
> *And is there honey still for tea?*

These lines were written in relation to a time just preceding the First World War, a time so far as the contemporary imagination is concerned when it was possible for

King's College Chapel, Cambridge

Jesus Green Lock, Cambridge

young 'gentlemen' to devote unrestricted days to strolling beside the river in the sun, not a few of them penning languorous verses as and when the inclination took them — only to feel the ultimate call of patriotism and rush off to sacrifice their lives in the trenches of Flanders and elsewhere. Both tranquillity and idealism permeated that era to some slight extent, and in Cambridge, despite the city's enforced succumbence to modernity, something of it lingers still. Brooke's evocation of the atmosphere of that now vanished era still holds much fascination. His affection for this area was clearly genuine, his ode on Grantchester describing the neighbourhood lovingly.

The enthusiast who has begun his journey along the Ouse at Bedford will find both the city of Cambridge and the Cam within its immediate vicinity quite different propositions. The same peacefulness however overhangs the river; nor is the Cam unlike the Ouse in its provision of waterside taverns, for at nearby Fen Ditton there is the excellent 'Plough Inn', its lawns sloping down to the water's edge, only just over three miles outside Cambridge and well rewarding both of the motorist's and the boatman's patronage.

It is certainly advisable to take some form of refreshment here, for travelling beyond Fen Ditton as far as Ely, with the exception of the recommended 'Bridge Hotel' at Clayhithe there are few provisions of this kind; only the gradual awareness as one moves forward of the feeling of Fenland becoming ever more pronounced, of the land remaining flat for miles at a stretch, water-free now and given over to agricultural enterprise but only a century ago water-logged, marshy and a positive haven for the fowler with his 'punt-gun' and the sedge gatherer, as at nearby Adventurers' Fen through which the Cam now flows just to the north of Cambridge. Distant 'isles', man-made river embankments and occasional clusters of trees provide the only relief to what would otherwise be monotonous scenery in every direction. Once one has regained the familiar flow of the Ouse two principal high-rises are visible over a good distance, that of Sutton-in-the-Isle and that of Ely itself, the former being the southernmost town in the 'Isle' of Ely and hence its name. Sutton does not lie on a waterway, though it is quite close to the New Bedford, on the opposite side of the water to Chatteris Fen, famous for its profusion of carrots. Ely of course lies conspicuously on the Ouse.

These two places have one thing in common, in addition that is to their both lying upon what passes for high ground in this part of the country. For when Alan of Walsingham built his magnificent octagonal lantern tower, Ely Cathedral's crowning glory and at the time of its construction the first such tower in England, he set a new fashion, one that persisted for many years. The village church of Sutton-in-the-Isle, dating from the fourteenth century, also boasts octagonal features, in fact a double octagon placed on top of its western tower. Certainly the influence of Walsingham's innovation is to be felt here, and indeed a similar feature

The Plough, Fen Ditton

The Bridge Hotel, Clayhithe

will be noticed yet again when the church of St. Botolph in Boston, Lincolnshire, is mentioned in these pages.

Sutton's church is a lovely structure, built at a time when the English Gothic had not completely developed but had nevertheless reached a point of satisfying excellence (alas, the church has been heavily 'restored', mainly during the nineteenth century). It is an extremely large church for what, at the time when it was conceived, can only have been quite a small community, though serving an extensive territory. To understand this phenomenon it has to be remembered that in Fenland the very existence of a patch of high ground invited ambitiousness of this kind, and the nearness of Ely Cathedral doubtless tempted village builders to emulate its grandeur as far as was possible. Today this fine church survives in almost enigmatic tribute to the sturdiness and steadfastness of those old Fenland citizens.

From Sutton it is possible to look out in several directions over the expansive, flat acres stretching far away beneath. Some feeling of the past awakens in one's imaginings, a feeling of gratitude that the ingenuity and tenaciousness of such men as Vermuyden has made it possible to visit or live in places such as this without either inconvenience or fear for the consequences. Descending to the flatland beneath, one feature, and one feature alone, commands one's attention: Ely Cathedral, surely among the handful of superlative ecclesiastical structures in this country. It and the hump of ground upon which it stands are visible for miles around.

The city of Ely is today a pleasant community; small by city standards, but quite large for the fens. William Cobbett, when he visited the city in 1830, had this to say: 'Ely is what one may call a miserable little town: very prettily situated, but poor and mean. Everything seems to be on the decline, as, indeed, is the case everywhere, where the clergy are the masters'. The once lovely cathedral he discovered 'in a state of disgraceful irrepair and disfigurement'. Happily the latter blemish has been attended to, though as is the case with all ecclesiastical structures of any magnitude Ely can hardly ever be visited when scaffolding is not visible at some point, either to assist in cleaning or else in renovation.

An earlier visitor than Defoe, Celia Fiennes, who made a tour through Britain on horseback, felt in 1689 that Ely was 'the dirtiest place I ever saw'. She had to contend with the frogs and snails that apparently inhabited her hotel bedroom; but when one considers the damp and marshy conditions then pervading this is hardly surprising. It was this marshland, centuries earlier, when it formed an eddying and highly dangerous swamp checkered by rivulets and quite isolating the Isle of Ely, that enabled the Saxon Hereward to hold out for so long against the Norman conquerors, that also enabled the monks of Ely to become rich and maintain their affluence in their isolated situation. Writing early in the seventeenth century Michael Drayton thus described the richness of the land:

40

Sutton-in-the-Isle Church

Of all the Marshland *Isles, I* Ely *am the Queene:*
For winter each where sad, in me lookes fresh and greene,
The horse, or other beast, o'rway'd with his own masse,
Lies wallowing in my Fennes, hid over head in grasse:
And in the place where growes ranke Fodder for my Neat;
The Turffe which beares the Hay, is wondrous needfull Peat:
My full and batning earth, needs not the Plowman's paines;
The Rills which runne in me, are like the branched vaines
In humane Bodies seene; those Ditches cut by hand,
From the surrounding Meres, *to win the measured land,*
To those choyce waters, I most fitly may compare,
Wherewith nice women use to blanch their Beauties rare.

It was during the second half of the seventh century that St. Etheldreda founded a monastery for both monks and nuns at Ely, and it is from this foundation that the present glorious cathedral finally arose. The lovely structure the visitor may inspect today was begun about the year 1080 — some years after Hereward's defeat — and building continued, as with many English cathedrals, decade by decade right up to 1322. In that year Ely Cathedral suffered a fate that seemed to blight so many such ecclesiastical structures: the great central tower collapsed. It was though but a signal for rebuilding, of adding even further to the outward glory of the structure; now Alan of Walsingham was enabled to construct his lovely lantern, already mentioned. Study the cathedral from a distance across the fens: it is a long building, the lantern midway along the line of the roof perfectly balancing the great west tower, a little taller than it. Regard the lantern from inside the cathedral, at the crossing, looking straight up: it is undeniably a magnificent achievement, its dimensions almost totally abstracted by the ingenuity of its design, itself demanding at the time of construction the utmost in engineering skill and inventiveness.

It would be wrong though to speak of Ely's octagon and nothing else. The cathedral possesses so many other lovely features; and, curiously, when one enters the building it does not seem as large as outward appearances would have one believe. Undoubtedly it is the great height of the nave and aisles which contributes most of all to this illusion. Nor, for that matter, can the cathedral be looked upon as Ely's sole attraction; though nobody would deny that without this building the city would hardly have advanced much beyond village status, a community the size of Sutton-in-the-Isle perhaps. The abbey gateway, Bishop's Palace and old school are all notable structures within the cathedral's immediate environs. The centre of the old city also displays many vestiges of antiquity; and down by the river there is a peacefulness rarely to be found in 'cities'. There are several reminders of bygone

42

Ely Cathedral from the Deanery

Ely, especially the fine old malting house, also a good waterside tavern known as the 'Cutter'. A well equipped marina is to be found here too.

Along this stretch of the Ouse Ely is undoubtedly the premier landmark; its cathedral, the present survivor of a past monastic establishment, stands as a reminder to those who are interested in such matters that at one time Fenland provided a veritable haven for men and women of a reclusive disposition, who wished to isolate themselves from society's more oppressive realities in order to devote their lives to contemplation and study, the nourishment of their own bodies by victuals raised by their own hands and to the worship of God. Or was that truly the case? Was there not perhaps avarice, hypocrisy and, specifically, lordship? At Ely, certainly, there are indications that at different times all of those traits were prevalent. Yet despite abuses of this kind, when Henry VIII dissolved the monasteries he at one stroke swept away a major aspect of British life and tradition. Those survivors of his energetic wrath examinable today, in however ruined condition, are most surely to be treasured.

The boatman or the motorist in search of waterside attractions is not concerned solely with historical associations however. From Ely the Ouse flows almost directly north to Kings Lynn, a town with as many historical associations as Ely, though they are perhaps of more recent vintage. Only one lock interrupts the journey north, at Denver Sluice, the first since leaving Earith. The River Lark joins the Ouse just south of Littleport; and that river is itself navigable for several miles, flowing as it does through Burnt Fen, Padnal Fen, Mildenhall Fen, and so on. It is typical Fenland.

Littleport commands one's attention on account of its having been one of the centres of what amounted to a 'peasants' revolt' in 1816, during an era—not only in the fens — when the disparity in wealth and living conditions between those who flourished and those who merely 'got by' was perhaps more marked than it has ever since been. Out of such rebellions sprang the seeds of Chartism, later trade unionism, later still of course Socialism. But the Fenland revolts of this period faltered and failed; principally because bemused, famished and misguided landsmen were not enabled to see beyond their immediate disgruntlements—a factor arising solely from lack of food. Looting, unnecessary violence and irresolution were the results; and the recriminations included the arrest, at Littleport, of something above seventy malcontents, the eventual deportation of six and execution of five of them. It was at Ely incidentally that these barbarous — at any rate un-Christian — sentences were meted out, in the name of the bishop of the day, who at that time possessed legal as well as ecclesiastical jurisdiction over his see.

Passing beneath Littleport bridge, along that stretch of the river now known as the Ten Mile Ouse, one encounters nothing at all save the usual expanse of rich, flat Fenland, a perfect example of the kind of terrain that has earned this section of

44

The Quay and the Cutter Inn, Ely

The Ship, Brandon Creek

Britain the proud title of the 'vegetable garden of England'. So it is; an unbelievably wealthy agricultural area, but one never free of the fear of flooding. Brandon Creek, whose 'Ship Inn' is illustrated here, presents the stranger with a name hinting at the tales of the old American west; but no such daunting history is attached to this spot, merely the recorded fact that the inhabitants of nearby Brandon, at the time of the main drainage of the fens, were fiercely opposed to the undertaking. Here also the River Brandon, or Little Ouse, meets with the Great Ouse, and he who can still find it in him to add extra Fenland miles to his log may sail upstream along the Brandon for a few miles with ease.

The Ouse's next tributary is the Wissey, and at the point where it joins with the main flow one passes into a stretch of the Ouse that until the last century bustled with comparatively heavy shipping. It is here that the Ouse acquires an entirely new character, linking its present guise with the industrial aspects of the eighteenth and nineteenth centuries; linking it too with Vermuyden's grand plan, as is borne out by the close proximity once again of the Old and New Bedfords, and most particularly with Denver Sluice.

There is something quite noble about industrial or mechanical landmarks of this kind. Denver Sluice, now linked with Downham Market by an unnavigable cut, stands as a positive monument to the vainglorious but on this occasion successful endeavour displayed by the rescuers of Fenland. A sluice is a floodgate, an outlet for over-high floodwater; that at Denver is one of the most impressive such structures in the country, dating from 1784, successor to an even earlier safety measure that proved less than a match against the floods of 1782, and itself greatly modified and sophisticated in recent years and now stretching over a considerable area.

From Denver Sluice, some fourteen miles away from Ely, one can still, if the weather is affable, view the long line of the superb cathedral. The contrast is piquant; and yet somehow the battle that has been waged in the fens over the centuries is summed up by these two remarkable man-made structures: the one a lasting symbol of human faith in an unseen power whose will can guide the motions of the climate, the other a more realistic edifice, a tangible attempt to come to grips with terraneous and climatic effulgences. Industrial archaeology has in recent years become an accredited branch of scholarship, as well as a popular form of distraction; Denver Sluice is certainly to be counted among the most interesting industrial, or at any rate mechanical, phenomena in eastern England.

The Wissey, which joins the Ouse just south of Denver, is navigable as far as Stoke Ferry, a distance by water of perhaps fifteen very winding miles, passing through the village of Hilgay. North of Denver Sluice, and just a little removed from the course of the Great Ouse, lies Downham Market, at one time, as its name suggests, an important trading centre. From thence, from nearby Salter's Lode lock, as far as Kings Lynn where the Ouse flows into the Wash, across terrain that at one

Denver Sluice

47

time was boggy marshland infested by multifarious currents, one is seldom forgetful of the vigorous mercantile activity of the past that although it no longer characterises Fenland can still be glimpsed to some extent at Kings Lynn, a town that presents the visitor with an array of lovely old buildings, many of them revealing the influence of Dutch architectural styles. Here indeed is a lasting testimony to the great volume of trade that used to be conducted between the two countries during the eighteenth and early nineteenth centuries, two countries which in the flatness of their terrain and the constant battles they have always been obliged to wage against the sea have more than mere trading instincts in common, more even than a mutually observed expansionist policy of utilising the sea and their own sea power.

The Ouse becomes gradually wider and deeper the nearer to Kings Lynn one draws; no locks now interrupt the tidal river's flow. Yet the vision of the past can only be partial, for the conquest of the fens has itself led directly to a diminution in the importance of Kings Lynn. The river is in no degree as much employed here as it once was.

To a far greater extent than Ely, Kings Lynn is one of Fenland's principal townships; its trading history extends back to medieval times, to an era when there were no fewer than three important trading guilds in the town, probably far more. Its prosperity continued throughout the sixteenth, seventeenth and eighteenth centuries, and there are numerous fine buildings that today contribute to the 'history in stone' of this unusual old town. There is still a flourishing harbour at Kings Lynn, immediately illustrating the source of all this prosperity and importance; and there is the Great Ouse stretching far away to the south and Ely, redolent of a past epoch when a flourishing river traffic was conducted along its waters to and from Kings Lynn, an arterial convenience that allowed Fenland to pursue the course dictated by its rich soil to the utmost of its abilities.

Kings Lynn's many fine buildings are worth outlining here, and perhaps the famous old Custom House. built in the eighteenth century to the designs of Henry Bell, is most apt to begin with. It stands overlooking the port it was built to serve, a lovely post-classical structure that immediately attests the great wealth which had become an integral part of the town's trading existence.

Bell was no mean architect, as this building amply demonstrates; he was also a man of substance and influence in the life of the ancient borough, and on two occasions he was elected to the office of mayor. It is said that he was the architect also of the 'Duke's Head Hotel', one of several large inns in the town built at different times to answer the requirements of visiting merchants.

It has already been mentioned that a considerable trade once existed between Kings Lynn and the Netherlands, and that a Dutch influence is to be detected in certain of the town's architecture; the old Custom House, with its ornately conceived roof, may certainly be counted among these buildings. A building that betrays no

The Custom House, Kings Lynn 49

evidence of style other than that of England is the superb hall of the Guild of Holy Trinity, built during the sixteenth century and displaying a lovely street frontage of chequered brickwork. There are many attractive old guildhalls and similar buildings scattered throughout the British Isles, and several are in fact older than this structure; it is though to be accounted easily among the loveliest and most interesting. It is of far larger dimensions than is at first apparent, and in fact this guildhall, which consisted originally of only a great hall built above a storeroom, extends back from the street a considerable distance; the main entrance way that covers the staircase leading off into the hall was constructed at a slightly later date, and proudly boasts not one but two royal coats of arms above its doorway, a circumstance arising from the fact that at the time when this addition was made the arms placed in position were those of Elizabeth I and then defunct. A royal decree necessitated the addition of a second coat of arms.

Today the guildhall is employed as town hall, thereby allowing it a fresh lease of life in a capacity not so very far divergent from that it was intended to fill in the first place. For throughout Europe guildhalls were erected to serve the social and financial requirements of groups of business people connected with a particular trade, and although the great medieval guilds themselves were by way of being private clubs it would normally be the case that members of local guilds were also the leaders of local society and government.

In a town like Kings Lynn, boasting many guilds, matters may perhaps have been a little less clear cut than this. An illustration of this circumstance is the fact that another of the old medieval guildhalls, that of the Guild of St. George, is still standing in Kings Lynn. There is, in this matter of guilds as well as in the general nature of the commerce pursued at Kings Lynn, a considerable resemblance between it and the historic town of Boston just across the treacherous reaches of the Wash, to be noticed in these pages over the next chapter. Like Kings Lynn, Boston also boasts a lovely old guildhall, and very much else of interest besides.

It is said that Wisbech, on the Nene, is the 'Capital of the Fens'. Ely, on account of its being a city, may possibly regard itself as having a right to claim that title; but surely if any one town should usurp Wisbech of its birthright in this respect it would be Kings Lynn. It stands imperiously at the south eastern corner of the Wash, an amazing testimony to the truth of the assertion that Fenland is affluent land.

CHAPTER THREE

The Witham from Boston to Lincoln

If Fenland may quite accurately be termed 'affluent' one portion of it, the northern fens, comprising the southern 'Parts' of Lincolnshire — Holland and Kesteven — curiously emerges, quietly, as being most affluent of all; affluent too in the unexpectedness of its physical attractions. People who live in London or in the south of England sometimes seem not to know where Lincolnshire may be found on the map. It is in fact the easternmost and largest of the counties in the Midlands; it is not, as many people seem still to aver, in the north of England. North Lincolnshire boasts its wolds, but its southern reaches are immediately identifiable as Fenland, and many of its extensive miles of waterway are navigable for pleasure.

To reach the mouth of the Witham, just to the south east of Boston, from Kings Lynn it is necessary to cross the Wash. Many people would be daunted at the prospect, and justifiably; it is possible to traverse the Wash in a small boat, though it would be ill-judged to do so without the assistance of a pilot, normally quite easily secured. There are very clearly defined channels to which one must adhere; banks of silt—themselves partially resulting from the determined drainage of the fens that has taken place over the centuries—exist in preponderance, and they in their turn contribute to the ferociousness of the current that is manifested here. The careful observer will already have taken note of the fact that the Bedford Rivers are tidal, feeling the merciless thrust of the Wash's daily turbulence and requiring the huge sluice at Denver, as well as many powerful pumps, to preserve an equable flow of water; he would do well, who wishes to cross the Wash, to bear this factor in mind, for it is an indication, albeit distant, of the untoward turn these waters may at a whim be mindful to take. The conscientious navigator will of course keep in mind the fact that to imperil his own life is at once to imperil the lives of those who will consider it their duty to attempt his rescue. Provided the proper channels are followed the Wash is easily crossed; if they are not, danger, lurking everywhere, will be swift to make itself apparent.

It may be worth pointing out here that only vessels of over fifty tons are legally required to seek the assistance of a pilot, and normally therefore official pilots are available for these craft only. Fortunately, local fishermen and others intimate with the Wash's crueller habits are easily secured and for a small consideration will see one safely across the water. They should always be sought out.

The Welland and Nene both give off into the Wash and will be discussed in their turn; the Witham may fittingly be considered before them, flowing through Lincoln, northernmost settlement in the fens, at least navigably speaking, and totally different from Ely, which it resembles in its possession of a magnificent cathedral church. Boston, after which town the lovely American city in Massachusetts is named, first greets the mariner who has troubled to cross the Wash from the south, just a short way up the mouth of the Witham. It is not such a large port as is Kings Lynn, but its history is just as illustrious and it boasts as many fine and famous buildings.

The 'Stump' immediately comes to mind, the parish church of St. Botolph and the largest such building in England, boasting an extremely lofty tower with a distinctive crowning 'pepper-pot'. This is a lovely building, and he would be curiously lacking in sensibility who did not succumb to its attractiveness. It, and the town of Boston, and the guildhall (now a museum) which is one of the borough's other principal architectural features, all claim intimate association with the Pilgrim Fathers; and as this town is so frequently visited by Americans, and the city which is named after it has developed into what is today one of the world's most prominent communities, it would be well to pause for a moment in order to consider the immensely significant events which led to the American city being so named.

First of all it has to be remembered that the Witham's outlet from the town of Boston into the Wash is both wide and deep, a natural port that has made ocean-going journeys from here easily possible. The Charles River, flowing through the American Boston, is a grander river altogether, but it gives an indication of why the English Bostonians and their associates selected that venue to establish America's first major city. Nor for that matter is the Wash altogether unlike Boston Bay, Massachusetts, in size or shape. There are a few mementos in the American city of this old English town; happily the lovely Georgian Fydell House, adjoining the guildhall of this English Boston, contains a room dedicated to the use of Americans, so constituted by the efforts of the late President John F. Kennedy's father when the latter was United States ambassador to the United Kingdom.

The guildhall itself is in truth a lovely building, although it is small. Here are to be found several reminders of those folk who sought to escape to foreign climes in order to avoid religious persecution and were as a result imprisoned in Boston to await trial in nearby Lincoln, at the other navigable extreme of the Witham. In the guildhall, in its capacity as a museum, one may inspect the doors belonging to the cells in which these sufferers were once incarcerated, in 1633; a plaque tells the story of their misfortunes. In part, the impressiveness of Massachusetts' Boston today stands as testimony to their faith and inventiveness. Paul Revere's 1775 cry of 'the British are coming, the British are coming' and the results of his famous ride inspire only the feeling that American revenge was just, a proper repayment for the suffering of many of the early settlers.

Boston Stump

Boston achieved prosperity during the fourteenth century as a result of the flourishing wool trade. By the eighteenth century the affluence which had for so long been taken for granted had for some reason deserted the town; it returned during the nineteenth century and is very much in evidence today. The lovely hall of the Guild of St. Mary, as at Kings Lynn but one of many in the town, reminds one forcefully of this early and fruitful concern with mercantile endeavour.

The Witham at Boston is of course tidal, and when the tide is out the bare clay banks of the river are not an attractive sight; they hint at prosperity having grown up about them *despite* their unpleasantness, *despite* the wrathful Wash to which and from which their waters run. The harbour, and the Boston quayside, present though a completely different aspect. Because their faces are of hallowed age they now seem curiously different from their own counterparts in such other ports as Grimsby, for instance; ports which seem curiously oblivious to the possibility of presenting a more agreeable appearance at the same time as being busy and efficient. There are numerous fine old commercial and industrial buildings along the Boston quayside and riverside, and at Bargate End on the east side of the river can be seen the nineteenth century Maud Foster windmill as illustrated here, unusual for its five sails. However, nobody would wish to deny that the 'Stump' is this old town's great glory, as it has been for many a year. No writer can better be summoned to evoke the grandness of this structure than William Cobbett, who visited the town in 1830 and wrote as follows: 'To describe the richness, the magnificence, the symmetry, the exquisite beauty of this pile is wholly out of my power. It is impossible to look at it without feeling, first, admiration and reverence and gratitude to the memory of our fathers who reared it; and next, indignation at those who affect to believe, and contempt for those who do believe, that when this pile was reared the age was *dark*, the people rude and ignorant, and the country *destitute of wealth* and *thinly peopled'*. Cobbett, who was ever one to tilt at windmills if he possibly could and who, unlike poor Don Quixote, occasionally managed to topple them, went on to compare the 'Stump' with St. Paul's in London, calling the latter masterpiece a 'great, heavy, ugly, unmeaning mass of stone' in comparison with the beauty of St. Botolph's.

Boston still presents the visitor with the spectacle of bustle, and it is attractive for it. Leaving the town and proceeding up river one begins at once to detect a great difference between the northern fens and those to the south of the Wash. Drainage still claims man's attentions, but there does not seem to be the urgency that there was and is elsewhere; this is somehow more amenable land, but possibly lacking something of the richness of the Huntingdonshire and Cambridgeshire soil. No longer is this the 'vegetable garden of England'. One is still far more likely to hear the reports of sportsmen's guns despatching flights of geese and duck than sounds of tractors busily planting and harvesting. And it is with this change of character in

Maud Foster Windmill, Boston

the land that one also perceives a difference in the people. It is averred that Fenmen are sturdily slow both in thought and word, but more often than not possessed of an almost sage-like natural wisdom. Immediately one thinks of those who dwell in the southern fens; for further north there is, at least on the surface, something more of briskness about the natives, perhaps a more pronounced awareness of the tenets of commercialism.

Before passing upstream along the Witham from Boston it should be mentioned that about the fringes of the Wash, just to the east of Boston, there are fascinating salt marshes that may be explored. Here plant life and bird life exist in varied profusion; indeed, the list of wildfowl to be found here at different times during the year, and particularly during the winter months, almost confuses one with its array of unfamiliar names: wigeon, brent, eider duck, shelduck, mallard, smew, goosander, scoter and pinkfooted goose. It is only equalled by the different kinds of grass to be discovered here.

These salt marshes extend right along the northern shore of the Wash and in time may well be reclaimed. Indeed, some reclamation is already under way in this area, at Freiston Point; and whereas until recently this spot was mere marshland, a century and a half ago it was widely popular for its sea-bathing facilities.

At Cowbridge, locks give off into the Medlam Drain, Cowbridge Drain (itself leading into Hobhole Drain, which in turn flows down to the mouth of the Wash) and other man-made waterways. These north Fenland drains in this pocket of land above Boston provide the adventurous sailor with a considerable mileage of navigable water. They do not however play any part in the overall plan of this publication, save to note in passing that they exist. Little of interest lines their banks; although the history of their construction is as fascinating as that of the Bedford rivers and other artificial cuts further south. At one time it was also possible to navigate the so-called 'Black Sluice' from Boston to the River Glen at Guthram Gowt and from thence to Spalding; just at it was possible to navigate the Sleaford Canal from Chapel Hill, eleven miles upstream on the Witham from Boston, as far as the town it was constructed to serve, still a handsome old market town. Neither of these waters is passable any longer; nor is the Horncastle Canal, flowing north from Chapel Hill. The Witham therefore is all that will be discussed here, more than thirty miles of it easily navigable between Boston and Lincoln, with only a minimum of locks to aggravate the not absolutely dedicated sailor and much interesting scenery in between.

At Dosdyke the Witham is joined by its tributary, the River Slea, which passes through the old town of Sleaford just mentioned and then later on its journey towards the Witham through the isolated Fenland village of South Kyme. This small village is notable for its twelfth century church, all that now remains of yet another one-time priory, and for a thirteenth century ruined keep. In the days when the nearby Witham served as a major link between Lincoln and the sea the priory at South Kyme would of course have enjoyed fairly easy communications with neighbouring communities. Indeed, as a result of this factor these northern fens were almost as heavily settled with monastic establishments as those further south.

The river flows straight and, for the most part, tranquilly. It is extremely popular with anglers; but for some reason, perhaps because anglers, although they relish their inn like anybody else prefer solitude, there is a singular paucity of waterside inns along this stretch of the Witham. A few miles upstream however, just removed from the river along its tributary known as the Bain, there is a village where the holiday maker will find a couple of taverns; he will in addition find there one of the most interesting old fortified structures in Lincolnshire. For this is Tattershall, whose castle (the keep being virtually all that remains of the original building) is among the gems of English masonry.

Before considering the structure itself the stranger would do well to gain access to its topmost quarter, and from there to gaze out over the surrounding countryside — Boston 'Stump' to his south and the huge mass of Lincoln Cathedral on its eminence to the north west; as well as villages in between and farmland of prodigious fertility, not to mention the fragmented ruins of the Cistercian Kirkstead Abbey. The Witham too may be observed from this vantage point, obedient and unharmful as it winds along, no more venomous an action in its mind than to flood a field or two should the weather become sufficiently inclement. It is vastly different from the Ouse about Earith.

Tattershall Keep, built to please the whim of Ralph Cromwell about the middle of the fifteenth century, its tower rising to a height of 118 feet, contains some of the finest early brickwork to be seen anywhere in Great Britain. The construction is said to have been undertaken by Flemish workmen brought over to this country especially for the purpose; it has benefitted from very careful restoration carried out during the early years of the present century at the instigation of that Marquess of Curzon who had but lately returned from his Viceregency of India only to be finally thwarted in his long nurtured ambition to become Prime Minister. If he had achieved nothing else he would at any rate be highly credited with this worthy undertaking.

Not the least of Tattershall's attractions are its external Tudor features in the shape of ornate window frames, while inside there are lovely old Tudor fireplaces. It is not at all difficult to imagine this keep in the days of the castle's splendour, when the outer walls were still standing and the name of Tattershall conveyed only the existence of a fortress, not as today of a village as well. At that time the keep's interior would have been richly hung with colourful tapestries, its rooms filled with heavy furniture. Outside, though, all was greatly different from the appearance of today, and not so very far removed in condition from the first castle to have been established here during Norman times. Then the Lincolnshire fens had not been drained; travelling conditions were difficult in the extreme; and most of the area consisted of marshland awaiting the enterprise of those who, later, would perceive the agricultural possibilities of this rich soil.

The Witham carries one further upstream to Lincoln, past the ruins of Kirkstead Abbey where the tombs of the Cromwell family of Tattershall Castle used at one time to be preserved, through Nockton and Branston Fens, the rising hill upon which the city of Lincoln is built visible in the distance. There is little to delay the traveller, save the reflections that must automatically accompany his tranquil passage hereabouts. This is still a virtually undiscovered part of Britain, a far cry from those stretches of waterway, already mentioned, between Bedford and Ely.

In employing the term 'undiscovered' however, it would be wrong to lose sight of the fact that the ancient settlement of Lindum, which is today Lincoln, was one of the major Roman strongholds when Britain formed a part of that impressive empire. It was to this part of England what York was to a slightly more northern clime. The Normans too were not slow to appreciate the merits of Lincoln's steep eminence, its easy accessibility to the sea by water. Both castle and powerful ecclesiastical see were established here. Perhaps to the traveller in the immediate vicinity the Roman influence is of more moment; for there exists a profusion of straight old Roman roads he may still motor along. The waterman in his turn may marvel at the fact that the old Fossdyke, running between the Witham at Lincoln and the Trent at Torksey, allows him direct access to rivers and canals that can transport him, if he so wishes, and if (in certain stretches) his boat is not too large a one, up into Yorkshire, across country to the west Midlands or even to London itself.

The Fossdyke will be discussed in its proper place, but first of all the wonderful city of Lincoln must be hastily explored. Indeed, he would be dullard who rested content with a mere glance at this city; for although like every other substantial community in the country it has been blighted with its fair share of ugly factories, three lane highways and huddled shops on the outskirts that seem to have no other purpose than to cast a cloud of depressiveness over what is otherwise attractive and yet at the same time appear to flourish, it somehow retains almost all of its antique loveliness.

Lincoln is a tourist's city; even so, only a very sturdily constituted visitor can negotiate its steep ascents and descents without tiring. One of the oldest streets is named 'Steep Hill', and the name is more than apposite. It leads one past a fascinating array of medieval houses and shops, many of the latter retailing either antiques or second-hand books, a haven for the curio hunter and a natural growth in an important cathedral city.

Having gained the summit of Lincoln's exacting hill the visitor is all at once presented with a number of fascinating buildings calling out for him to examine them. The cathedral beckons most insistently, but the castle should not be

Lincoln Cathedral from the Waterside

neglected, even though little remains other than the massive curtain walls and impressive entrance. Unusual to Lincoln is the fact that numerous civic offices have been established in buildings standing within the castle grounds, including the courthouse.

The cathedral defies the praises of one whose task it is to describe only briefly the places of interest to be encountered along the principal waterways of Fenland (indeed, some may even declare that it is fanciful to include Lincoln within the fens). However, when John Ruskin opined during the last century that St. Hugh's cathedral was one of the definitive gems of English architecture, not merely it will be noted of medieval architecture, he was by no means understating his case; even though the Victorian sage was given to dogmatic assertions that, many of them, can today be brushed aside with but a snigger. Few cathedral facades can surpass the west front of Lincoln; nor can any church in this country equal the magnificence of this structure when it is viewed from a distance, its great length and its massive towers quite dominating the city which has grown up around and more particularly beneath it. This masterpiece of church architecture, begun in Norman times but requiring several centuries to complete owing to continual development and such accompaniments to church building as toppling towers and caving roofs, is one of the glories of the English Gothic architectural style. The fens are rich in ecclesiastical structures, both large and small: Lincolnshire itself, county of 'spires and squires', is blessed with a wondrous variety of parish churches; Ely and King's College Chapel in Cambridge and other buildings have already been mentioned; Lincoln Cathedral, surely, overshadows them all.

Parts of the old Roman wall still stand in Lincoln, and in the Newport Arch one is still able to inspect the original north gateway to the city; curious little houses strike one at the turn of every corner, displaying half-timbered features, rickety gable ends or — in two instances — those chimneys placed over front entrances that are a mark of a house having once been inhabited by a Jew. There are several worthwhile inns and eating houses in the city, but there is one establishment of a quite different character that the discerning visitor should not on any account miss, and this is of course the Usher Art Gallery and Museum.

It comes perhaps as a surprise to find an extremely good collection of paintings in a small provincial gallery (including works by Sickert and other members of the modern English school of painting), but there are two special collections contained in this museum, both of them devoted to men associated with Lincoln and the surrounding area, that are of especial interest. The first is a collection of Tennyson memorabilia, the second an extremely wide-ranging collection of works by the painter Peter de Wint. To describe these collections, or to enter into biographical details of the two men concerned falls beyond the scope of this short book, but by any standards both of these collections are important, to the curious and to the student alike. Tennyson, it will be recalled, was born in the rectory at Somersby in Lincolnshire in 1809; while de Wint, despite his Dutch name, was born in Staffordshire in 1784 and did much of his finest painting in and around Lincoln. Some of his small sketches for large subjects on display at the Usher Gallery inspire one with feelings of extreme envy and admiration.

The Lincolnshire poacher is one of English folklore's most immediately memorable legends, even though its origins are not very old at all and it has been mainly propagated by the catchy tune that everybody today knows. A Lincoln inn can however boast a fine association with just such a gentleman, and it would be wrong not to recount the circumstances here. The public house in question is the somewhat macabrely named 'Strugglers Inn', the final calling place of those unhappy sheep stealers and other contumacious offenders destined for a hanging death nearby. It possesses, in a glass case once displayed on a wall but subsequently removed to a cellar, a stuffed dog of the whippet variety. The dog apparently once belonged to a local poacher whose name, variously spelt, was Malik Devaner and who will be mentioned again in these pages in connection with another public house. It often happens that local hearsay embodies the vestiges of truth, and so this may indeed have been the poacher's dog; though whether he was the actual poacher who gave rise to the famous song the present writer is not in a position to say. This particular poacher, enjoying the protection that arose from warm local affection, did not suffer the fate of so many similar wretches; instead of being hanged after he was finally brought to trial, he was deported, and after several years of exile succeeded in returning to his native country. He died only in 1927 and is buried in a local churchyard.

In order to pursue this poacher's story a little further the river traveller has but to steer his craft away from Lincoln, away from its alas somewhat muddied waters, desert the Witham and pass along the old Fossdyke. The Romans built their roads straight, and although the maps show this to be a stretch of water with several twists it nevertheless amply demonstrates that they were equally capable of cutting straight stretches of canal. Halfway between Lincoln and Torksey lies a village with a name hinting at pre-Norman origins — Saxilby. But before even this is gained, a matter of only a couple of miles outside Lincoln there stands beside the canal — or 'river' as the local people prefer to call it — an old-established inn with the unusual name of the 'Pyewipe'. This inn has been conducted by members of the same family for well over a century now, and in earlier times it was no more than a small, common alehouse serving passing bargees (today it serves golfers and fishermen, in addition to summer sailors). It was here, so local tradition has it, that the poacher just mentioned made his headquarters, and indeed it is not difficult to conjure up an image of this old inn a century ago, removed from the main road by half a mile of trackway, providing ample security for such an offender as he. Mercy never has been

The Pypewipe Inn and the Fossdyke, Lincoln

shown to such outlaws in Britain, once captured; the clemency shown to this personable malcontent is still surely deserving of congratulation. If the voyager has time to pause from the musings he will undoubtedly find it necessary to indulge over the original Roman paving that can still be perceived on the bed of the Fossdyke as it flows by the 'Pyewipe', he could do worse than contemplate for a few seconds the unhappy end of so many other Lincolnshire poachers. Those wretches hanged at Lincoln were buried in a separate corner of ground just inside the castle walls, and it demands little of anybody's reflection to spare a thought for their unconstructive punishment.

Most people who pass along the Fossdyke will be making for the Trent and such interesting towns through which it passes as Newark or Nottingham. The bounds of this book do not extend beyond Torksey Lock, where the Fossdyke ends, an almost miraculous survivor from ancient times. The Dyke is only some eleven miles in extent, and yet its function today is of unsurpassable value to the tourist. If he has not paused at the 'Pyewipe', therefore, where his requirements would have been more than adequately seen to, the visitor should tie up his boat at Torksey, where at the 'Hume Arms' he will find what is indubitably one of the finest hostelries in the entire east Midlands, famed far and wide for its good food and its carefully tended decor.

This fine old inn derived its name from the Hume family of Torksey Hall, now no more than a ruin opposite. On the banks of the Trent close by, though, there is a far more impressive old survivor: that of Torksey Castle, once painted by Peter de Wint. With this the consideration of the Witham and the Fossdyke must close. For convenience's sake, it will be imagined that the sailor decides to make his way back to Lincoln, from thence along the Witham to Boston, and so once more into the Wash.

Before passing from this area however, and taking leave of the Witham, it is worth recalling one or two facts and figures likely to throw some light on the character and history of Fenland. From Boston to Lincoln, by river, is not very much above thirty miles; the Witham itself is almost seventy miles in length. More pointedly, the total number of acres of Fenland drained by this river, through the agency of sluices, cuts and pumps, is above a quarter of a million. Drainage has perhaps reduced the dimensions of the Witham along its navigable stretches, for remains of very large ships of ancient times have been uncovered from land now standing quite high above river level. This in itself is an indication that Lincoln was an extremely important settlement in Roman and post-Roman times; it gives also a hint as to the way in which the character of the landscape has altered over the centuries. Fortunately — at least marksmen will have it so — there is still plentiful marshland in the immediate area, where duck and other wildfowl exist in abundance, especially within the area surrounding the Wash. Wildlife generally flourishes, and the bird-watcher is as amply catered for as the sportsman, the angler and the sailor.

One other point is deserving of mention, and as the Wash is to be referred to once more it is perhaps apt. It has been inferred that the Witham was once a far wider and far deeper river than at present, just as the Great Ouse was to the south of Kings Lynn. Just beyond Boston is a part of the Witham mouth known as the 'Haven'; in days gone by, before drainage and reclamation had been fully implemented, the land about Bicker, today several miles removed from the water, was known as 'Bicker Haven'. A pub in Bicker, the 'Old Red Lion', used three centuries ago to be called the 'Seaman's Rest'. If anyone doubts that a great struggle was once waged in order to wrest land from the sea let him take out his atlas and compute the distance between Bicker and the Wash, and then remind himself that what is today dry land — albeit insecure — was once water. Perhaps less dramatic than the victories further south, this is nevertheless a salutary observation.

CHAPTER FOUR

The Welland from the Wash to Stamford

It is only a short distance along the edge of the Wash from the mouth of the Witham to that of the Welland, one of the most typical of Fenland waterways but alas no longer navigable along its entire extent. It is a shame that this should be so, for the historic town of Stamford lies upon it, and could at one time be reached by river. Not far from its mouth the Welland is joined by the Glen, which is also navigable only for a very short distance now, not even as far as the important market town of Bourne any longer. Nevertheless, there is some good sailing along these two waters, and they certainly must not go unmentioned in these pages. Nor for that matter ought it it to be forgotten that Spalding, tulip capital of England, lies on the Welland. Before the traveller between Witham and Welland decides to pass into the latter, though, let him recall the charge given earlier in these pages: the Wash is dangerous water, and even for so short a distance as this it is advisable to secure the assistance of a pilot.

The following lines, once again by Michael Drayton, writing in the seventeenth century, serve even to this day to define the atmosphere of this central Fenland area. They are well worth pondering:

> *Through Quicksands, Beach, and Ouze, the Washes must she wade,*
> *Where Neptune evry day doth powerfully invade*
> *The vast and queachy soyle, with Hosts of wallowing waves,*
> *From whose impetuous force, that who himselfe not saves,*
> *By swift and sudden flight, is swallowed by the deepe,*
> *When from the wrathful Tydes the foming Surges sweepe*
> *The Sands which lay all nak'd, to the wide heaven before,*
> *And turneth all to Sea, which was but lately Shore,*
> *From this our Southerne part of Holland, cal'd the Low,*
> *Where Crowlands ruins yet, (though almost buried) show*
> *Her mighty Founders power, yet his more Christian zeale,*
> *Shee by the Muses ayd, shall happily reveale*
> *Her sundry sorts of Fowle from whose abundance she*
> *Above all other Tracts, may boast her selfe to be*
> *The Mistris, (and indeed) to sit without compare,*

E

And for no worthlesse soyle, should in her glory share,
From her moyst seat of Flags, of Bulrushes and Reed,
With her just proper praise, thus Holland *doth proceed.*

To consider first of all the Welland, whose source lies near to where the Civil War battle of Naseby was fought, and whose course takes it by so many places of historic value and interest; close to the park of the lovely Elizabethan Burghley House, for example, an ostentatious but at the same time incomparably lovely stately home built by Queen Elizabeth I's favourite in the expectation that she would visit it frequently, which as it transpired she did not. Burghley House is today so wealthy in works of art that it rivals many excellent art museums.

Beginning the journey inland from the Wash one passes first of all through Fosdyke (not to be confused with the Fossdyke described in the previous chapter); thence, having passed by the influx of the Glen, a straight line leads towards Spalding, through Spalding Marsh and its flat and somehow damply unappetising land. This is tulip territory; each year in the late spring tourists come by the thousand to inspect the acres upon acres of these colourful flowers — better in quality, it is said, than those grown in Holland; and different from them as well, for whereas most of the tulips grown in Holland are for the purpose of selling as bulbs only, many of those in the Lincolnshire fens are destined to be sold simply for decorative purposes. Even so, how many tourists pause to consider that the potato is a vastly more important agricultural feature in this part of the country than the tulip, and that far more land is given up to cultivating it.

There is no denying that in season these tulips provide an impressive vista. Normally they are in full flower during the first or second week in May, which is slightly early in the year for the boating enthusiast in this area. To commemorate the harvest the citizens of Spalding have, since the Second World War, been in the habit of holding an annual tulip festival. It is on a much smaller scale than many better known floral festivals, but not the less impressive because of that, the colourful floats decorated exclusively with tulips, fashioned in all manner of shapes and patterns, being an apt reminder of the acres of red, yellow, white, orange and otherwise many hued flowers that certainly impress the passer-by with their intense richness. To pass among them by slow moving boat would surely be a memorable experience. Nor do tulips provide the market gardeners of the Spalding area with their sole source of livelihood: daffodils and other spring flowers are to be seen here earlier in the year.

It is worth noting that the channel of the tidal Welland that carries it from the town of Spalding to the sea is artificial, having been formed during the third and fourth decades of the nineteenth century — by a process of reinforcing the banks of what was then known as the 'New Cut', and narrowing the central channel of water — to enable shipping to pass easily to and from Spalding. As with many enterprises, owing to eventual lack of funds the good work evidenced at the outset was allowed to deteriorate into a sorry condition (the artificial banks themselves having been formed by nothing more sturdy than thorn faggots interwoven and naturally reinforced by the silt carried with the tide), and towards the close of the nineteenth century it was found necessary to undertake further extensive improvements. It was the same old story, the age-long story of Fenland; so that in 1882 W. H. Wheeler, an engineer, was able to record in a publication devoted to the subject of Fenland drainage, dealing specifically with the Welland overfall: 'The arterial drainage of this district is still very defective in condition, the channel not being sufficiently adapted to carry off the rainfall as rapidly as it is collected in the river. The banks which protect the fens are constantly being broken, owing to the channel being overfull and the fens flooded. The repeated floods of the last few years have done an immense amount of damage by submerging the land and destroying the crops'. One wonders how frequently since then words precisely similar to these have been uttered. Certainly they were spoken many a time earlier, for even the Romans, as elsewhere in the fens, were active in the drainage that was necessary here both in order to establish good communications and to further the cause of agriculture.

Despite the immense volume of agricultural industry which it has to support, Spalding is a peaceful little market town, its tranquillity disturbed only on festive occasions and during that period of the year when the tulips are in bloom. It boasts many fine old eighteenth century buildings, and the lovely fifteenth century riverside Ayscoughfee Hall, now the property of the town. The Welland has always been deep here, and earlier river activity is easy to imagine.

Ayscoughfee Hall, dating from 1420 and featuring some lovely gardens, is of considerable interest for its association early in the eighteenth century with one Maurice Johnson, one of the founders of the Society of Antiquaries in London and an early member of a club known as the Spalding Gentlemen's Society. Such provincial gatherings of cultured people were quite numerous during the 'Age of Reason'; that at Spalding is markedly unusual for the fact that it survives to this day — even though it is a far cry from the coffee-house and tavern bonhomie characteristic of Maurice Johnson's time and so specifically associated with that literary namesake of his who earlier had lived just off London's Fleet Street.

Although the Welland is not officially navigable beyond a point seven or eight miles west of Spalding, it is worth following it as far as Stamford; for not every Fenland enthusiast is a sailor and the river has much to offer in the way of picturesqueness, and around Stamford it is immensely popular with the fishing fraternity — fishing, so it is said, being the most popular sport in Britain. There are in addition several worthwhile pausing places, and numerous facilities for the yachtsman.

Crowland, or Croyland Abbey is the first historic relic of interest one comes across. Little remains now; but the story of the abbey's founder, one Guthlac, is full of intrigue. As a young nobleman he was something of an outlaw, but rather of the Robin Hood variety than any other, returning to its rightful owners so legend has it one third of whatever he had stolen from them. Like so many before and after him, he duly experienced feelings of severe remorse for his lawlessness; unlike so many who know not how to reform and who thus continue with their lawbreaking for want of any other pursuit, the young man entered the monastery at Repton where he acquired the rudiments of sanctity and learning.

A life of solitude was a natural step from this; but few men would have elected, as did Guthlac, to come and live among the damp marshes of Fenland, alone on the isolated isle of 'Croyland'. Under the patronage of Ethelbald, King of Mercia, in the year 699 Guthlac established an abbey here. Later buildings naturally followed, and a fire of 1091 necessitated the complete rebuilding of the church, the Normans having by this time taken possession; but as with all other establishments that were not saved through being created bishoprics, the abbey fell into a condition of dilapidation following the dissolution of the monasteries in the sixteenth century. To the visitor today it stands as yet another reminder of the immense steadfastness of faith that must have accompanied the resoluteness of those medieval ecclesiastics, when complete isolation and harsh privation for the greater part of each year was the only kind of existence to be won of the fens.

Crowland, even though it is largely a ruin, is still employed as a parish church; and somehow its semi-ruined condition only adds to the impressiveness of its aspect. The village of Crowland is notable for a most unusual fourteenth century triangular bridge that once crossed the Welland but does so no longer, the abbey church for the magnificent frame of a great west window, flanked by statuary, that still stands beside the present west entrance to the church, itself characterised by what can only be described as a squat steeple. The following lines, from a verse preserved in manuscript form in the British Museum, apply to Crowland in its monastic days:

> *In Holland in the fenny lands,*
> *Be sure you mark where Croyland stands.*
> *Croyland wine is but so-so;*
> *Sedge instead of hay doth grow;*
> *A bed like stone whereon to lie.*
> *And so begone, without 'good-bye'.*

Beyond this lovely grey-stone village, through what is called Borough Fen, lies the small village of Peakirk. The marshy Fenland has of course always been a haven for wildfowl, and nearby are the so-called 'Waterfowl Gardens', administered by Peter

Crowland Abbey

Scott's Wildfowl Trust. At Peakirk too there is an aptly named inn, the 'Ruddy Duck'; even if one is unable to pass this far any longer by boat, at least the motorist may pause to appreciate the fare at this excellent establishment close to the river.

The next two places up river are Deeping St. James and Market Deeping, both of them long-established communities and still exuding something of the placid quietude of the Fenland of yesteryear, when bargees providing their not over-hurried transportation were often enough the only strangers the inhabitants would encounter from one week's end to the next; bargees, and perhaps occasional merchants on brief visits from the larger towns, all of which possessed large hotels which were erected during the eighteenth and early nineteenth centuries as the then modern equivalents to the medieval coaching hostelries, of which many have happily survived throughout this country.

It was from Market Deeping eastwards on its journey to the Wash that the intemperate Welland had to be artificially channelled in order to assist shipping and land drainage. Officially, its name over this stretch is the 'New Cut' or 'New River', but normally, as in these pages, the name Welland is retained. If one is travelling east it is at Market Deeping that the fens properly speaking begin in this area; fittingly it was from this town, during the reign of Edward the Confessor, that a timber road was laid down stretching as far as Spalding, then a town situated much closer to the sea than is the case today owing to the great volume of land 'reclamation' that has taken place in succeeding ages. Fittingly also, even during Norman times strenuous efforts were made to quell the ferocity of the undisciplined Welland that flowed in a hazardous direction and flooded potentially rich fields as often as it was allowed to do so. It was Richard of Rulos, the Conqueror's agent in this part of the country, together with the Abbot of Crowland, Ingulphus, who initiated a policy calculated to subdue the terrain hereabouts. This, it should be remembered, all took place during the eleventh and twelfth centuries. The process continues to this day, with arable land still being claimed acre by acre from an unwilling sea.

A few miles more and one gains Stamford, almost in Rutland and itself graced by that lovely grey stone which is such a feature of England's smallest county, one alas, of several which after a gallant struggle, are now destined to disappear, at least for administrative purposes. Stamford boasts so many attractions and associations of interest that it is difficult to know how to catalogue them. Nearby Burghley House, home of the Marquess of Exeter and one of the loveliest Elizabethan residences anywhere in England, has already been mentioned. The Soke of Peterborough is soon to disappear, and when that occurs the house will stand in Huntingdon-shire — at least a portion of it will, for under the new arrangements the boundary of Northamptonshire passes right through the property. Its treasures exist in such profusion that it is impossible to describe them here; but it should be mentioned that

Stamford from the River

an even earlier residence stood upon this site before this house was built; and even before that time, it is thought, a monk's cell was established here.

Contrary to what the term might seem to convey, a 'cell' was not the abode of a hermit, but an establishment usually presided over by one monk who had been despatched from a parent abbey to oversee its landed interests in some other part of the country, normally close by but sometimes far-flung. Perhaps this cell was an offshoot of Crowland, or of Thorney, or of Spalding where there was also a monastery, or even of Peterborough.

Stamford itself has of course long been an important ecclesiastical centre, famous for its numerous spires all visible from a distance, famous too for the loveliness of much of its architecture. The town is itself old-established, and at one time appeared set fair to rival the two university cities of Oxford and Cambridge in its academic significance. The reason for this is not difficult to ascertain; for although Stamford was an important settlement even in pre-Roman times it was with the Norman conquest that it became a flourishing township. Monks and friars of every order and avocation came here, and the churches to be seen in Stamford today all stem from their activities. It was the accompanying prosperity of the cloth industry — its development not unassisted by the convenient Welland — that drew them.

Where there were monks there were also flourishing centres of learning; schools were established, and finally, during the reign of Edward III, at the behest of certain Oxonians who had disassociated themselves from their parent college and found refuge at St. Leonard's Priory, a new university was suggested, and actually started. Ultimately, as might have been anticipated, the authorities at the two premier British universities objected and the foundation came to nothing. One can but speculate upon the situation today if this institution had been permitted to flourish and there was another medieval university in existence in such close proximity to Cambridge. Certainly the appearance and atmosphere of this town on a hill, with its ancient buildings, its sloping narrow streets, its antique and low-beamed inns and taverns and its many churches, is conducive to studiousness and the advancement of cultural pursuits.

Possibly the most lovely of Stamford's churches is St. Mary's, with its fine spire added a full century after the building's initial completion in the thirteenth century. Inside this church is a monument to that William Cecil who built nearby Burghley House, also monuments to his parents and to several other members of the Cecil family. Stamford possesses as well a fine town hall and a lovely old bridge across the Welland — a more recent and much more convenient method of crossing the water than the paved ford that is said to have been laid down here in Roman times.

According to Daniel Defoe Stamford was once accorded city status, only to be sacked by the Danes soon after the departure of the Romans. Even today it would be well worthy of the description. It claims one further distinction: of having been a main resting place on the Great North Road during the great age of coaching. It still boasts old inns that a century and more ago were dedicated to travellers' needs, either in providing them with rapid refreshment while new horses were obtained for their coaches or else in seeing to their overnight requirements. Until comparatively recent times the Great North Road still passed through the town, tortuously; today Stamford has been by-passed, and by early evening each day, once the shops have closed, it assumes a gentleness that it probably did not know even two and three hundred years ago, at a time when the next important town on the road north — Grantham — meant several hours of uncomfortable riding in a coach, instead of half an hour's rapid driving along a dual-carriageway as is now the case. Like nearby Stilton, which has virtually ceased to exist as a sleepy village but which once flourished, Stamford can today enjoy the reward of peace, in recompense for its busy past.

Stamford lies as far upstream on the Welland as this book may run. It is necessary now, therefore, to pass back along it, seawards, as far almost as Fosdyke, to turn into the even more tranquil river Glen. Few people living without the immediate vicinity of this waterway have ever encountered its name, and yet like the Welland which enabled Spalding and Stamford to know prosperity (particularly the former, for Stamford has always enjoyed good road connections) it too once bestowed significance upon what might otherwise have been a totally overlooked Fenland community.

Like the Welland, the Glen has presented drainage experts with many a problem over the years. Today it is calm. One may pass up it perhaps as far as Pinchbeck, and then down to a point just south of Bourne where the so-called 'Bourne Eau', now no longer navigable, joins with it, which during a past epoch gave Bourne an easy access to the sea. Just before this, at Guthram Gowt, the 'Black Sluice' (the 'South Forty Foot Drain' of the 1630's) runs off north, and then wheels round to the east as far as Boston, itself being joined by the 'Clay Dyke' to the old Sleaford Canal, as already mentioned a sadly neglected artery. None of these is now in use, though it is a great pity that this should be so, and perhaps with the contemporary surge of interest in waterways the matter may soon be rectified.

Recalling both navigational and drainage requirements throughout the ages, in this instance more particularly the latter, perhaps of even greater poignancy is the continued existence — and use — of the old Roman 'Car Dyke'. It runs from the Witham just east of Lincoln, not so very far away from the Fossdyke already referred to, south to a point below Bourne. Today it is but a flood bank, but originally it was an important channel, its fifty six miles calmly drawing water from the hills to the west directly into the Nene, thereby avoiding the danger of Fenland flooding.

Since Bourne is the last place to be mentioned in this chapter, it would be well to say that although it is a typical Fenland market town, but a shade of its former self as far as the waterways are concerned, it is still a very flourishing community indeed. Good roads and fast motorcars have naturally done for Bourne to some extent precisely what they have done for other towns of its size. As far as the tourist is concerned, however, it still lies off the beaten track; which may be taken either as a godsend or a shame according to the turn of individual minds. Historically it has much to offer, from the attractions of the old 'Angel Hotel', a coaching inn of a past age, to the nearby ruins of Bourne Abbey, yet another reminder of how very intent the monks of Britain once were to sever themselves from the cares of the everyday world, to establish their own communities in far-flung and isolated places, whatever the consequent hardships. Apart from a few crumbling stones belonging to ruined domestic buildings , only the abbey church remains standing at Bourne. This abbey was founded in 1138, possibly by Hugh de Wake whose family claimed associations with the Hereward who had provided William the Conqueror with such opposition.

Bourne can lay claim to one other interesting, even if somewhat macabre association. At one time the rector here was the father of that Doctor Dodd who was hanged in London during the lifetime of Doctor Johnson for his fraudulent actions in obtaining money. For a clergyman to suffer this ultimate penalty was at the time considered a dreadful circumstance, and every effort was made to secure his reprieve, Johnson playing an active but not altogether optimistic part. A remark the great doctor made with reference to the wretched cleric's imminent execution has passed into the annals of quotation dictionary compilers and exchangers of maudlin conversation in public houses. 'Depend upon it, Sir', Johnson pontificated in the presence of his friend Boswell, 'when a man knows he is to be hanged in a fortnight, it concentrates his mind wonderfully'.

Bourne Abbey, therefore, is one more to be added to the tally of Fenland monastic houses, one more reason for condemning the avaricious destructiveness of Henry VIII. Fortunately the town itself has survived in good order, even if it no longer has a direct water link with the sea.

CHAPTER FIVE

The Nene Old and New

The Nene also gives off into the Wash, as do all Fenland waterways directly or indirectly. Since the Wash is a general point of interchange for all Fenland navigators who may wish to sail any distance, explore more than one stream and its tributaries, it will perhaps be forgiven if once again it is imagined that a course is being pursued upstream rather than downstream.

In many ways the Nene is the most interesting of all Fenland rivers, even if for much of its extent it does fail to provide the picturesqueness one associates with certain stretches of the Ouse. For one thing it passes through the town that is generally called the 'Capital of the Fens', and for another it is at least as intimately associated with the maze of man-made rivers as is the Ouse, its own original course now being more generally classed not as a river but as a navigable canal, flowing through such places of interest as Ramsey and March, both of them extremely important centres in the past. That, for the purposes of this book, the upstream course of the Nene concludes at Peterborough, whose cathedral presents the visitor with the third ecclesiastical wonder to be seen in the fens, is an equally important fact.

The Nene's story should first be touched upon, for much of the navigable stretch that bears this name today is not the original river at all. The reason is elementary: the land that lies between the Nene and the Ouse, the new Nene that is, is all reclaimed land, surrounded by marshes. Today when people talk of the Nene they refer exclusively to its new course, and in these pages as a result it is necessary to think in terms of two distinct rivers, which is indeed the case.

The Nene rises deep in the Midlands; beginning at the Wash it is navigable in a westerly direction as far as Northampton, and from there, by means of a short artificial channel, it is possible to pass into the Grand Union Canal and, if one has a mind to do so, to travel as far as London. He who shoulders the task, however, would do well to consult his charts in advance and consider the number of locks he will have to negotiate. They are numerous, almost a hundred between Blisworth and the Thames at Reading.

It would be impossible to recount the story of the Nene's present course in this short narrative; but it is worth keeping in mind when one pauses to consider the vast expenditure that the sea and her rivers have exacted of man over the centuries in

Fenland that even in the 1820's the sum of £130,000 had to be budgeted in order to erect a new embankment near what appears on the map today as Sutton Bridge, together with the straightening of the Nene in this vicinity. They were heady sums even to such businessmen as the Duke of Bedford and his successors.

For nearly thirty miles inland the Nene is tidal; almost to Peterborough in fact. The boatman should take the necessary precautions, especially the nearer the Wash he is. Sutton Bridge is the first place he will strike, lying in the Holland division of England's second largest county, Lincolnshire. The land hereabouts is marshy, offering but mild attraction to anybody other than the marksman and the dedicated agriculturalist, or the ice-skater during the winter. It lies nearly ten miles from Wisbech, and over the course of those ten miles one might almost be passing from one country into another; while a similar observation could be made about those ensuing nineteen miles separating Wisbech from Peterborough.

Beyond Sutton, whose citizens have ever since the seventeenth century witnessed an immense struggle against the elements, there lies a further stretch of deep and rewarding water. Rich agricultural land may be seen on either side; and the stranger, especially if he has navigated hither from more northerly and un-arable climes, should not neglect to pay at least momentary attention to this circumstance.

At Wisbech he may rest content, having at last arrived at Fenland's 'capital'. Why this town should have the acclamation — and not Boston, or Kings Lynn or even Ely — at first appears something of a mystery, the community's centrality seeming to be the crucial factor. But once again one has to consider a past era, a time when the sea extended further inland, when this bustling port with its wide and deep harbour facilities was much nearer to the Wash. Today, as well as being a busy port still, it is a picturesque old town, and the association with King John, who dared the marshes about the Wash to evade his pursuers, is still of great intrigue to the romantically disposed. The possibility of the immense fortune that the monarch is supposed to have lost while negotiating this tricky terrain being still likely to come to light deep in the clay is still occasionally advanced. But although it has its devotees the expectation seems somewhat fanciful, for even assuming that the treasure might once having existed it has to be taken into account that the action of the sea would over the years have either ensured its being buried beneath layers of silt or else being swept entirely away. Nor for that matter would it be an easy matter to assert with any degree of accuracy just where King John crossed: two thousand years ago, for instance, the Wash stretched twenty miles further inland than it does today. In all likelihood John and his followers crossed at a point quite close to where Wisbech is built today; and although tradition has it that they crossed by foot it is more likely that they in fact employed boats. That was in the year 1216, and poor John was destined to die only a few days afterwards. If after almost 750 years any booty he may have been carrying with him has survived it would be virtually miraculous;

Peckover House, Wisbech

however, the lure of treasure-trove remains, and the school of thought which has it that the treasure still exists will doubtless always persist.

Wisbech's importance stems from the fact that it is a port, and in the past it was an extremely busy one, rivalling Boston and Kings Lynn in the volume of its trading. Like these two associated ports, it was at one time one of the country's principal centres for the importation of wine from the continent of Europe; during medieval times it also had very close ties with the trading towns of the Hanseatic League. This one-time bustle has now partially deserted the town, leaving behind an air of antique sleepiness in certain corners, itself mingled with the hint of olden grandeur manifested, as with so many other Fenland communities, in the large old hotels and stately residences of the merchant classes. Peckover House, built about 1722 and illustrated here, is perhaps pre-eminent among her Georgian domestic buildings, now in the care of the National Trust. Today, as some form of recompense, Wisbech is also an agricultural centre, and an extremely prosperous one. Among its many attractive features is the parish church dedicated to St. Peter and St. Paul, notable mainly for the profusion of different architectural styles to be examined both inside and out, and for the supposed date of its first building — the year of the four ones, 1111, so it is said, though definite proof would be hard to establish.

The stretch of the Nene running from Wisbech to Thorney, some fourteen miles, is one in which a gradual transformation from starkness to relative luxuriance is to be observed in the terrain and its growth. It is still very much Fenland; indeed, like so many other places in this part of the country, Thorney was itself once described as an island. As with many similar locations, the surrounding grimness and barrenness induced monks to found an abbey on the spot, adding yet another to the extraordinary number of Fenland ecclesiastical establishments of this kind.

The island of Thorney was the property of the old Saxon Kings of Mercia, and it was one of them who originally granted the site to the Abbot of Peterborough, who in turn despatched certain of his monks there to lead a life of solitude and devotion. As was only natural, the establishment grew. Then, during the ninth century, it was sacked by invaders from Denmark. Fortunately it was rebuilt and prospered a second time, notably during the reign of the saintly King Edgar. A new church was built, but in 1051 it was pillaged by Earl Godwin, being rebuilt in 1085. It is this lovely old Norman building that can still be examined in part at Thorney, a pleasing reminder of the time when this particular religious establishment was considered to be of such importance that its abbot was allowed the dignity of wearing a mitre, thus placing him on the same footing as a bishop. 'Thorney the flower of many fair tree', runs an old jingle, and there can be no doubt that many such abbots ultimately lived extremely easy-going lives, pampered by the luxuries and extravagances that accompanied accession to great wealth. In this respect Henry VIII was perhaps right to condemn the monasteries; to have dissolved them, as he did, simply out of

Thorney Abbey

maliciousness and greed, was surely unforgivable, the cause of irreplaceable losses in the medieval architectural heritage of Britain and a not inconsiderable blow to the progress of learning and the patronage of the arts. Like so many other one-time monastic centres, Thorney is today a fairly insignificant village; the water that at one time surrounded it and made it necessary for boats to be employed in order to support communication between the old abbey and its parent establishment at Peterborough has now been drained away. Because of this the village now no longer stands beside water, the Nene flowing by two or three miles away.

` The boatman may perhaps baulk at traversing this short distance by foot; he would do well though to visit the old abbey remains. But if it is merely refreshment he seeks at this stage in his journey, and the opportunity to pause awhile, he need look no further than the riverside 'Dog in a Doublet' public house at Northside, the nearest point of access for Thorney. Here he will find a widely celebrated hostelry, one that claims to be the only public house in the country bearing this name and one that is prominently marked on all the boating maps. How this fine inn obtained its name is a mystery to the present writer; but perhaps all the same local traditions have survived to explain it, while the inn's sign provides some clue. For although one side of the signboard has a depiction of a huntsman with a small dog peeping out from inside his doublet, the reverse side, the original, portrays a dog actually attired in a doublet. The visitor must make his own choice.

A name, though, is of no avail in attracting custom; only excellence of cuisine and pleasantness of surroundings can do that. The 'Dog in a Doublet' may be confidently recommended. It is a pleasant occupation to while away an hour or two in such congenial surroundings before passing upstream to Peterborough or downstream to Wisbech. There is an excellent restaurant also, for those who do not reject the idea of attiring themselves in something at least slightly more sartorial than shorts and singlet when on a boating holiday. Finally, it must not go unmentioned that this stretch of the Nene is extremely popular with fishermen, and this is as much a haunt of the fishing fraternity as of boating enthusiasts.

There is a lock to pass through here; thereafter five uninterrupted miles separate the 'Dog in a Doublet' from the city of Peterborough, until the new county boundaries are introduced the principal built-up area in its own 'Soke'. Few English sokes have survived even up to their imminent disappearance as decreed by a decision at Westminster, and it is thus pertinent to enquire the meaning of the term soke. On the face of it the answer is simple. Soke, or 'soc', is an old and wholly English word meaning a franchise (as applied to land); land, in other words, held by socage. It is a legal expression, and it embodies the notion that the administrator of a soke holds certain powers of administration that in earlier times would normally have been associated only with a feudal or manorial lordship, or, in more recent times, a county and its council. As maps once indicated, the soke of Peterborough used to

The Dog in a Doublet, Northside

enjoy what virtually amounted to county status. If further elaboration is required, it might be mentioned that the word soke is closely allied with the words 'sake' and 'seek', both of which in their original usages were legal terms denoting plaintiffs' or defendants' 'cases' or 'causes'.

In approaching Peterborough the visitor would therefore do well to consider the antiquity of its now extremely rare administrative status. Musings such as this will naturally be swept aside once this same visitor catches sight of the remarkable cathedral (now in danger of being all but swathed by a hideous encirclement of office blocks), but they hold a kind of interest even so.

Before passing to a consideration of the cathedral itself — which is really the only reason for visiting Peterborough today, unless one is travelling by train and is required to bide awhile at the station in order to achieve a connection— it cannot be left unsaid that what must at one time have been a lovely old city has been irreversibly disfigured in recent years by the decision taken by what used to be known as the London County Council to use it as a 'London overspill' town. Large complexes were accordingly planned, negotiated, constructed; new housing estates were established. A considerable body of industrialists opted to take advantage of the situation thus handed to them gratuitously — thereby themselves helping to disfigure the old town — but apparently there were not enough of them, and the scheme has somehow been suffered to remain suspended in mid-air. Such is the situation at the time of writing, and Peterborough, although it offers every amenity imaginable and boasts excellent shopping facilities, really has nothing to offer the sensitive visitor other than its lovely cathedral. The boatman is perhaps a little more fortunate, for there is delightful meadowland through which the Nene passes close to hand.

Like that at Lincoln, Peterborough Cathedral boasts three towers; yet here they are so positioned as to have allowed originally for the addition of a fourth. The fourth was never added, but nobody who views the cathedral from the west could fail to doubt that it was indeed planned originally; moreover, only by such an addition would the abstract composition thus presented appear complete and almost totally satisfying. Of further pertinence is the assertion that almost certainly, had the lovely Norman building continued according to its original plan, all four towers would have borne spires. Then the illusory geometric perspective of the structure as viewed from ground level would have been complete. Even if all these spires had been set in place they would not alas be satisfactorily visible today, 'developers' having conspired together so successfully to obscure the building.

Peterborough is of course still famous for its bricks, and the high chimneys belonging to the brick manufacturers hereabout are landmarks for miles around. As the boating enthusiast approaches this old city it will be these stubborn structures he first picks out in the distance. Fortunately brickwork is not in evidence in the

Peterborough Cathedral

older buildings in the neighbourhood, and the cathedral is constructed throughout from fine Barnack stone.

Like all medieval cathedrals in Britain, that at Peterborough was originally a monastic church. Sir John Betjeman has somewhere written, in his at once immensely enthusiastic manner, that the difference between English medieval cathedrals — that is monastic churches — and ordinary parish churches of the same era is that the former constitute 'architecture' whereas the latter embody mere 'building'. Allowing for the numerous exceptions that everybody could cite, there is much truth in this. Monks conscientiously raised buildings to the glory of God; and although it may be opined that they had little else with which to fill their days and little else upon which to spend their money, they were responsible for the three cathedrals at Ely, Lincoln and Peterborough mentioned in these pages. When one considers that Fenland is such a small area, and that possibly only four other cathedrals in the entire country can match these three—Wells, York, Durham and Gloucester — the immense richness of this area in this respect becomes apparent. If one wishes simple sailing, accompanied only by the frenzy of busy river traffic and unadulterated commercialism, one goes automatically to the Norfolk Broads; if one wishes to avoid the more blatantly unpalatable trappings of that once delightful corner of the country, and relishes peaceful scenery with the convenience of exceptional nearby amenities, one perhaps takes a trip on the Thames; if one harbours any feeling for the past, as well as for the individual character that of course attaches itself to any part of the country but which in Fenland is enhanced by comparative lack of spoliation, then this area holds out numerous attractions. In Peterborough, with its excellent cathedral, one finds yet another reason for making this claim. That the destroyer of monasteries, and with them much of their fine church architecture — King Henry VIII— should also have a close connection with this surviving establishment adds piquancy to the state of affairs, as well as a feeling of sadness. Inside Peterborough Cathedral is the tomb of Catherine of Aragon, divorced wife of Henry and hapless victim of political circumstances making it necessary for the King to produce a male heir. Mary, Queen of Scots, was also buried here, but her remains were removed to Westminster Abbey in 1612.

If it might appear that undue stress has been placed in these pages upon the ecclesiastical structures to be discovered in Fenland, let it be said at once that their numbers well warrant it. A word too must be said of scenery; for once Peterborough is reached, travelling west from the Wash, it alters altogether. In truth, this is no longer Fenland. As far as the Nene is concerned, this Fenland river meanders as far as Northampton, and with the inconvenience only of a number of locks it is undemandingly navigable that far. It passes beneath the Great North Road, the A1 near the one-time Roman camp of Castor, and with this location this narrative must take leave of the Nene as it flows today, casting a final look in the direction of an

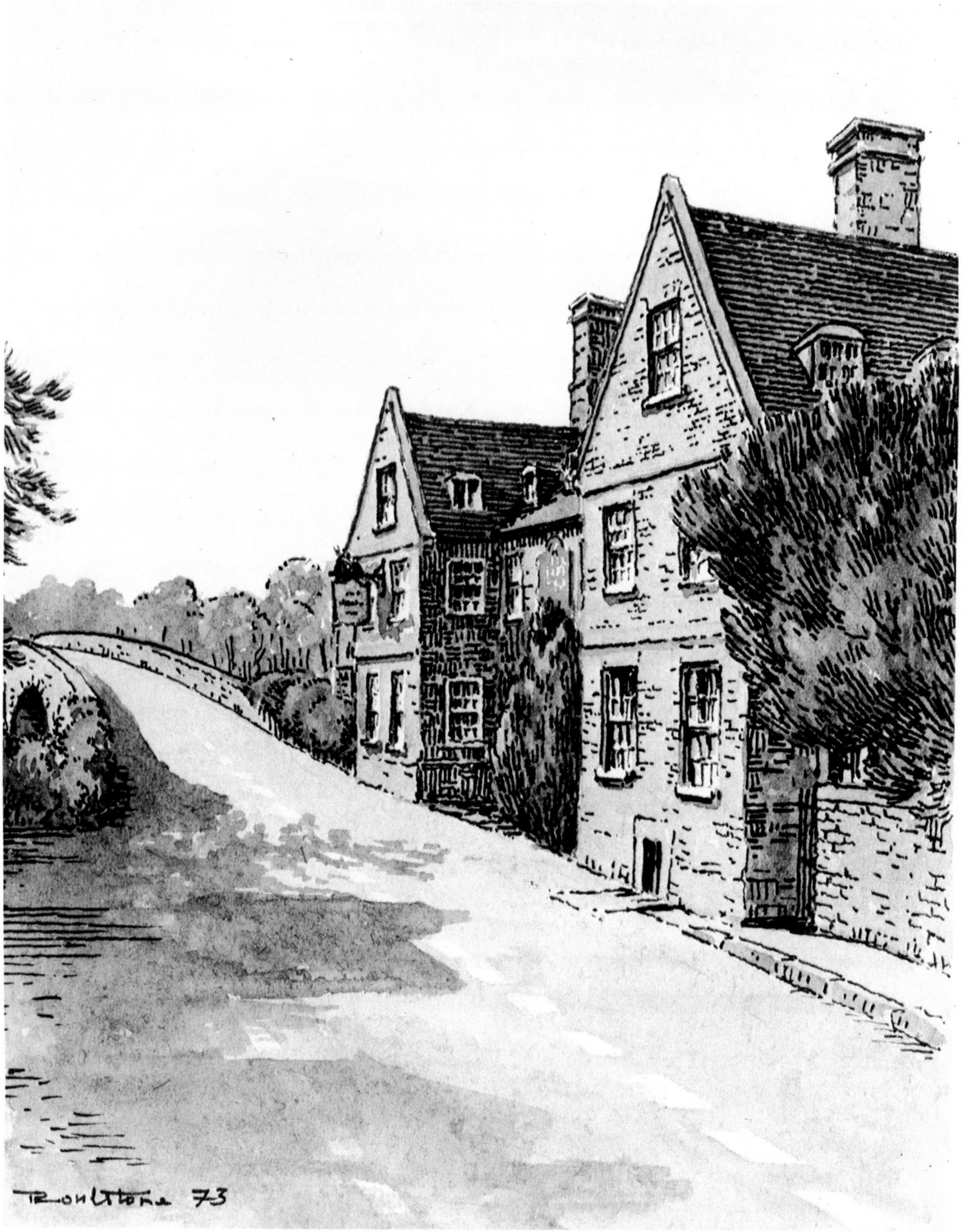

The Old Haycock and the Bridge over the Nene at Wansford

establishment lying just a few yards to the west of the Great North Road in the village of Wansford, the fine old 'Haycock Hotel', still the most prominent building in this village. Like Stilton, Wansford, a little to the north, owes its one-time standing almost wholly to the age of coaching, to an era when the 'Haycock' was a principal calling place on the road to and from the north. For the motorist of today it is so still, for there is easy access from the highway. To the boatman also it offers many attractions, while the Nene here is quite delightful. To reverse the procedure employed elsewhere in this book, contemplating this noble river as it flows seawards, not vice versa, it is almost as though, as it passes through Wansford, it is still unaware of the less malleable adventures awaiting it when it nears the Wash. Here it flows through meadows, not through expansive flat fields filled with root crops; here also it meanders, it does not proceed monotonously straight, subject of tidal manoeuvres and silt-bank lurches as it approaches the Wash, where more likely than not it will be obliged to assume a brownish colouration in keeping with the clayey soil through which its present course has been cut. This silt, by the way, observable within the immediate vicinity of the Wash, has over the centuries assumed such a tenacious hold upon the soil it influences perpetually that layers of it, indicative not so much of tide after tide but rather of year after year, are easily discernible in the very top-soil of the land merely by placing a spade in the ground and displacing soil to the depth of one foot.

The Nene between Wansford and Northampton is a totally different Nene from that between Peterborough and the Wash; just as the Ouse between Bedford and Earith is quite different from the Ouse that flows from thence as far as Kings Lynn. Many a holidaymaker will not care to travel much further east by water than Peterborough, and that is his right of choice. But in closing these pages it may be worthwhile tracing the Nene's course to the east once again, this time following an entirely different route, that described still by the old Nene. It is a separate waterway altogether, today virtually a canal, its passage governed exclusively by a series of locks and sluices, themselves firm reminders of the eddying and marsh-infested torrent that once constituted the Nene, indeed that co-mingled it for long portions of the year with both the Welland and the Ouse, as well as with the encroaching sea. This course, navigable for many miles, from Holme to Outwell, where a false channel conducts it down to Denver Sluice and so to the Ouse fourteen miles south of Kings Lynn, is of immense interest. Apart from the fact that it conducts the traveller through such antiquity-pervaded communities as Ramsey and March, it also takes him through the very heart of that part of southern Fenland that embodies so much of the history of the struggle, occasional defeat, eventual victory and permanent threat characterising this part of Britain, country that still echoes to the name of the once despised Dutchman Vermuyden, who despite the disfavour he met with during his own lifetime may yet be regarded as the true architect of

Fenland reclamation. The Old and New Bedford Rivers have already cropped up in these pages; the old course of the Nene flows more or less parallel with two other slightly less grandiose channels, but just as important in their own way: the 'Twenty Foot' and the 'Seventeen Foot', both deriving their names from their widths. The famous 'Forty Foot' cuts from west to east nearby. Other, no longer navigable channels once joined the old Nene with the new Nene at Wisbech and the 'Seventeen Foot' drain with the Ouse only about three miles south of Kings Lynn. If anybody doubts the immense labour and bitter endeavour that went into the drainage of the fens let him read H.C. Darby's book on the subject. There the story is set out with lucidity; and in many ways it could be said that the history of Fenland, until comparatively recently, could be divided into two distinct categories: land drainage and ecclesiastical devotion. It is almost as simple as that; save for the fact that always there have been ordinary Fenland dwellers, cutters of reeds who travelled about in small boats, cattlemen who passed almost all their days guarding their kine from the waters, fishermen, bargees who conveyed vast cargoes of merchandise from the larger inland towns mentioned in these pages to and from those important ports about the Wash. As the fens were slowly tamed these bargees gradually plied an even greater volume of trade; today they are not called for in significant numbers, but even so one frequently sees barges passing slowly along the Bedford Rivers, or one of the many 'drains', carrying fuel oil to the automatic pumping stations without which Fenland would once more become a heaving mire of marsh and mud. Sometimes it is an almost frightening thought.

Further north, in the area immediately to the north east of Boston, something similar is in evidence, but it is in the area of the fens between Earith and Peterborough, between the course of the new Nene and the Ouse, that this aspect of Fenland is best epitomised. The small pumping stations are not so conspicuous upon the horizon as the old windmills once were; but they are still extremely necessary, and thankfully they do their job more efficiently than the windmills did.

Before following the course of the old Nene the town of Whittlesey must be mentioned. It lies just south of the new Nene's course, not very far from the 'Dog in a Doublet' at Northside. Whittlesey Mere, with which the name of this old town is still associated (alongside the curiously named 'Ugg Mere') was at one time a lake, a permanent expanse of water contrasting with the more temporarily water-covered territories now known as fens. One would need to acquire an entirely new vocabulary in order to come to grips with all of Fenland's lore; but with Fenland meres being meres no longer the task is made doubly difficult, requiring almost archaeological instinct. Whittlesey, though, is a town which should be visited, its association with Fenland drainage extending back several centuries.

With mention of meres the following, final lines by the admirable Michael Drayton may be quoted, for they give the flavour of seventeenth century Fenland:

Of sundry Meres *at hand, upon my (Ely's) Westerne way,*
As Ramsey Mere, *and* Ug, *with the great Whittlesey:*
Of the aboundant store of Fish and Fowle there bred,
Which whilst of Europes *Iles Great* Britaine *is the Head,*
No Meres *shall truely tell, in them, then at one draught,*
More store of either kinds hath with the Net been caught:
Which though some pettie Isles likewise acknowledge me
Their soveraigne. Nor yet let that Islet Ramsey *shame,*
Although the Ramsey-Mere *shee onely gives the name;*
Nor Huntingdon, *to me though she extends she grounds,*
Twit me that I at all usurpe upon her Bounds.

They give too a proper demonstration of the essentially limited area to be defined as 'Fenland'.

Close to Holme, where this narrative begins again, is the famous Holme Post. In 1851, at a time when the people in the area most concerned with the problem of peat shrinkage were beginning to realise that they were dealing with a matter of serious and indeed intractable size, they made the experiment of sinking an iron post which had been a part of the structure of the Great Exhibition in London of that year and measured some twenty two feet in height. They sank it completely in the peat, its base purportedly resting on clay. One hundred and twenty years later, owing to shrinkage, some twelve feet or more of this post stand above ground. Possibly it is no longer a matter for undue alarm, but facts such as this certainly speak for themselves, and Holme Post can do no more than stand as a warning against taking too much for granted.

From Holme the 'New Dyke' takes one to the eastern end of the 'Forty Foot', which in turn gives access to the Old Bedford. Ramsey lies a mile south, one more of those Fenland towns that at one time boasted a flourishing abbey. This establishment has been even more unfortunately treated over the years than its counterparts at nearby Crowland and Thorney, for at Ramsey little remains of the old abbey, simply the partial ruins of its church, close to a river that no longer possesses very much importance but can still provide the tourist with much pleasure. The beginning of the old Nene's present deflected course is to be found only just beyond Stilton on the old Great North Road, and so it is remarkable that such a comparatively lengthy stretch of it should be navigable at all in fact. Again, as one looks out over the fens at Ramsey, due east in the direction of Chatteris, across acre upon acre of rich soil that produces so many of Britain's domestic vegetables, one cannot help but wonder at the Benedictine monks who had the temerity to settle here; or at the immense achievements of those whose professed aim it was to drain the fens.

The Gatehouse, Ramsey Abbey

89

From Ramsey one passes directly into the main course of the Nene, a desperately winding course which gives one some indication of how untamable this area must have been in centuries past. All is flat; there is little to observe. The raised banks of the 'Sixteen Foot' and the 'Twenty Foot' are visible to right and left respectively. During the winter, whipping winds race across this open flatland with unbelievable ferocity, to such an extent that flying top-soil can appear as a low cloud from a distance. In ancient times the inclemency of the Fenland winter climate must have been hard to contend with, and one wonders how livings were ever made.

The river flows close to Benwick, held to be Fenland's most prosperous village, one moreover that received mention in Domesday Book, the only community in these so-called 'Black Fens' to do so. The word black refers of course to the colour of the soil, whose richness is responsible for the prosperity of such places as Benwick. The Nene's old course continues from here along its winding way, no longer obliged to seek out its own passage seawards as was once the case. A few miles on it is joined by the so-called 'Whittlesey Dyke', and then continues on to March, another of Fenland's major townships and one more of those one-time 'islands' that for so long and so fastidiously retained the identity they possessed before the drainage of the fens.

March is not a large town, and among its very few interesting buildings it can claim little other than the church of St. Wendreda, with its superb hammer-beam roof and its carved angels attached to it in such profusion, a veritable 'angel host'; yet prosperity has long been in evidence here, and it cannot be denied that this is a typical Fenland community. It has never of course enjoyed much importance as a principal river-trading centre; it is a purely agricultural place, a market town, one of only a handful of such significant towns to be found in Fenland: St. Ives, Ely, Ramsey, Chatteris, Wisbech and March. Ask the average resident in southern England where these places are and he will probably be unable to give you an answer. Perhaps he will have an idea that Ely is an island somewhere off the east coast. He will not trouble to reflect that, but for the agricultural endeavours of those who live in the farms and villages surrounding these towns, many of his staple foods would be far more expensive than at present.

Barges carrying out essential duties connected with drainage, fishermen, children in dinghies, skaters in winter taking advantage of the frozen, still waters, a few holiday boats; such is the tally of activities now associated with the old Nene. Bird life flourishes also, which makes it popular with ornithologists. The old Nene is connected with the 'Twenty Foot' a little beyond March, with 'Popham's Eau' further on still, which in turn connects it with the 'Sixteen Foot'.

'Popham's Eau' is a significant stretch of waterway, in that it is named after a one-time Lord Chief Justice of England, who about 1605-10 was very much concerned with the problem of drainage in this area. He and his colleagues, who for their outlay in both brain-power and hard cash stood to gain something in the region of 130,000 acres of rich agricultural land, such as is visible hereabouts today, were responsible for many cuts and projected cuts in the Wisbech area. Among them only 'Popham's Eau' is navigable today, and then but for a short stretch. During the seventeenth century Londoners and others knew the geography of the fens; at any rate a few of them did, and they hoped to reap immense fortunes from their knowledge.

Just beyond the connection with this 'Eau'— a term found more frequently in northern Fenland than in the south — one strikes Marmount Priory. A lock named after this foundation alone stands as a reminder of its one-time existence. Where there are locks there are variations in land level, and yet again the observer is forced to recognise the fact that during the very early middle ages whenever a piece of high ground showed its head in the fens, even if only a few feet above water level, it was seized upon and colonised by those of a reclusive disposition, be they monks or nuns — and initially, as at Ely, they combined together (although at Ramsey women were strictly outlawed, regarded as objects of peculiar disdain and never allowed even inside the abbey).

Beyond here there is but little of the old Nene. At Upwell one is reminded of the fact that in days long since past, when the Ouse also flowed in this direction, before it was diverted to join with the Old West, before the construction of the Old and New Bedfords, it was here that the Nene met up with the Ouse. Because of flooding, their courses were seldom delineated with any degree of clarity, but this was so. An old canal now joins nearby Outwell with Wisbech; alas it is no longer navigable. The present-day navigator is obliged, once he has passed through Upwell, to steer now in a south easterly direction, along the seventeenth century aqueduct to Well Creek which crosses over the now unnavigable section of the 'Sixteen Foot', down to Salter's Lode lock and the Great Ouse just south of Downham Market near Denver Sluice.

The names of these various man-made phenomena are redolent of an exciting era. They all stem from the time of Vermuyden's activities, and it is perhaps instructive to glance rapidly at some of the precursors as well as survivors of this flurry of reclamation, to remind oneself of the dates involved. Since this narrative has now arrived back at a point dealt with earlier — the Bedford Rivers — it may be allowable to include in this very brief consideration the whole of Fenland.

The Old Bedford was cut in 1637, the New Bedford in 1651. The new course of the Nene was cut at various times, but the principal among its stretches, that between Peterborough and Guyhirn, which flows past the 'Dog in a Doublet', was set out in 1728. Several decades separate the two. Yet Moreton's Leam, which still exists but is no longer navigable, covering virtually the same ground as the Nene along this stretch, slightly to its south, was cut between 1478 and 1490. The 'Twenty Foot' was cut in 1651, the 'Sixteen Foot' in the same year, the 'Forty Foot' likewise. These last three were all part of the same reclamation scheme that also produced the New Bedford.

The fifteenth century has just been cited, and it has already been mentioned in these pages that in many areas of Fenland the Romans actively attempted something in the way of drainage; but with the instance of the Nene outfall being cut only in 1830 and the Ouse outfall, the so-called 'Marsh Cut', dating only from 1852, one gains a concise and bewildering impression of the fearful struggle that Fenlanders and Fenland 'adventurers' have been called upon to endure. The pleasure-cruising sailor of today, as he manoeuvres his craft along these deceptively calm waters, would do well to keep dates such as these in mind. Nor should he forget that tempestuousness of the elements, such as is occasionally manifested, can still cause both havoc and the headache of considering fen drainage anew.

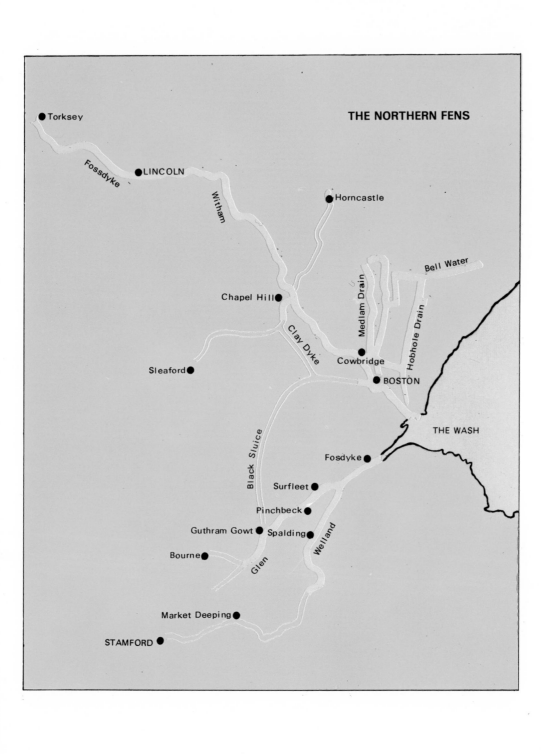

THE NORTHERN FENS

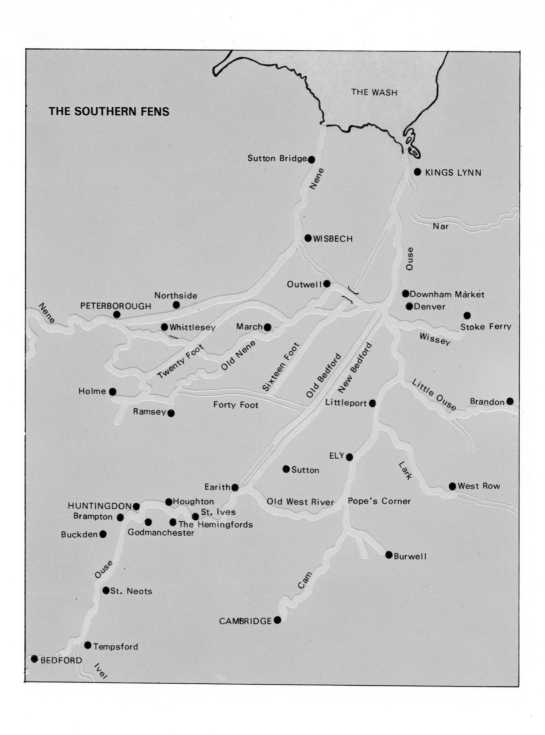

THE SOUTHERN FENS